INFLUENCER INCOME

Influencer Secrets to Profit and Prosper in the Golden Age of Social Media

JASON CAPITAL

Any questions about the book, rights licensing, or to contact the author, please email: jason@highstatus.com

Book cover and interior design: Andy Meaden meadencreative.com

ISBN: 978-1-54399-939-6 Paperback

CONTENTS

1 THE GOLDEN AGE

Dan Bilzerian is pointing a gun at me.

I'm sitting in Dan's living room.

We're talking about social media over dinner.

Dan is asking me a question, but the gun he's been playing with for 20 minutes is now pointing directly at me.

Dan realizes this and points the barrel elsewhere, as I do my best to explain my discoveries with social media.

(The gun was unloaded. I think.)

These last few years on social media have taken me to a lot of strange places.

In the beginning, I swore I'd never even use social media.

When Nataly (my girlfriend of 6 years) first showed me Instagram, I told her, "I will *never* be on this app. I will never be an Influencer".

Today, 3 of my companies are built solely on the foundation of social media. At least one person calls me an Influencer every single day. And I use something called the Influencer Engine to drive all of it.

If social media disappeared tomorrow, my companies would be fine but the transition would be no fun.

So I don't "like" social media today.

I love social media, because I've found I use social media very *differently* than any influencer, guru or social media expert I've ever met.

To me, social media is not social media.

Social media is business media.

(My initial feelings toward social media changed when I realized this little fact.)

Social media is distribution, indoctrination and conversion.

We're literally talking about free distribution for our brand and message, to scale our income and our impact. What's not to love?

In every other decade since the invention of marketing, you had to pay for the distribution and eyeballs we now get for free.

Today it's free to post, to share, to let our message be heard, and yes, it's even free for us to sell and monetize.

Once I saw that, I saw amazing businesses can be built by anyone using social media. Even you.

I have a friend who grew his coaching business to $10 Million a year using only social media and the Influencer Engine. (His profit margins are very healthy.)

I have another friend who helped a supplement company grow to over $100 Million a year using only social media and the Influencer Engine principles.

I have a 24-year old student who as a "solopreneur" is generating $150,000 a month now selling physical products with only social media (he doesn't even have a website).

I have another 28-year old student who became a millionaire this year selling education in the trading industry. All of the revenue was driven, for free, using social media and the Influencer Engine.

And I have hundreds of students who are successfully helping local businesses reach more people, get more customers and earn a whole lot of Influencer Income using only social media and the Influencer Engine.

What's amazing is that there are no "Influencers" involved in these traditional businesses yet the principles work just as well. (These traditional businesses include but are not limited to real estate agents, restaurants, daycare centers, doggie daycare centers, gyms, spas, chiropractors, anti-aging centers, and nail salons.)

Social media's not *going* to be big.

It is big.

In fact, it's huge.

The most recent survey I saw had the average person spending 2 hours and 22 minutes a day on social media.

That's not including Internet use.

That's strictly "time spent on social media".

And it's not just teenagers. The 35-44 demo is currently spending 2 hours and 4 minutes a day on social media. The amount of time spent has increased every year for 7 years now.

My buddy has a 16-year old. He says her and her friends still turn the TV on at night but they don't watch TV anymore. They watch YouTube.

(My buddy is 48. He watches YouTube at night too.)

Look around you. What do you see most people doing?

They're on their phones. Plugged in. To social media.

For my fellow entrepreneurs, we are officially in the Golden Age of Social Media.

Welcome.

If you're still in the stands and not a "player" on the field yet, it's time for you to get off your butt and get in the game. It's time for you to get your slice of Influencer Income from the multi-billion dollar Influencer Pie. This book will show you how (and save you several years of failures and costly lessons I paid for in cash, time and ego bruises).

If you're already on the field and in the game, this book may be even more important for you. It will show you how to get a lot more out of what you're already doing. (I've consulted or partnered with some of the biggest Influencers online today. I've yet to find one who was tapping into the true potential of their brand. From my vantage point, Kylie Jenner is probably the only one and she's got a lot of help.)

And it doesn't matter if you're on every social media platform, or just one (or none yet).

Everything I'm going to share with you in this book applies.

As you apply it, you'll find your account starts to get more engagement than most, if not all, of your competitors.

You'll notice that everything you create, everything you share, has more influence with your audience than ever before. (We can't *impact people* if we can't *influence them.*)

As a result, your account will begin to drive more traffic, get more customers and drive more profits than ever before. (This is my promise to you, and I insist you hold me accountable to this promise throughout the entirety of this book. Deal?)

In this book, I'm also going to show you a new way to monetize any social media audience, including yours, using a secret weapon called the Chat Engine.

You know how nearly every social media allows you to have private conversations with your followers? (Instagram calls it DM, Facebook Messenger calls it PM, and so on.)

Most Influencers use this feature to connect with their audience when followers message them, which is great.

But what they don't realize is those messages aren't just messages. They're leads. And no business worth its salt would ever ignore *inbound leads*, right? Amazingly, this is what most brands and Influencers are currently doing: Ignoring inbound leads.

Understand: We are in the Digital Age, and this is the Conversation Era.

You and I don't talk on the phone anymore like we used to. We text and chat.

Our audience is no different.

They prefer to text and chat.

Every single one of my social media accounts generates 6-figures a month or more, using only the Chat features, on the various social media platforms we're active on but it didn't start that way.

When we first realized all those people messaging us were leads, the lights went on. It was "found money". A brand-new profit stream that grows larger every month.

This "profit stream" is sitting inside your account right now too. (I'm going to show you how to make it yours using something we dubbed the "Chat Engine" in Chapter 13.)

Just to give you a taste of what's possible, and you may think this is small or large, a buddy of mine with 250,000 followers on Instagram recently reached out to me.

He wanted my team to apply the Chat Engine to his account for him, including all the software we built that really makes it go.

I was busy writing this book while running my companies and almost told him no. Then I thought, well, if we do it and it works, it'll make a great case study for the book. So I told him we'd test it out but I wasn't sure if it would work because we'd only applied it in-house to our own accounts.

What were the results?

Before he partnered with us and the Chat Engine, his Instagram made him about $5,000 a week.

In the first 7 days, our system drove an extra $54,000 in revenue from his account, selling only his own products. (The same ones he was already selling.)

In the first month, it drove an extra $121,000.

The Chat Engine should add an extra $1,000,000 or more this year to his top-line, almost doubling his business.

He was sitting on a social media goldmine.

Since then, I've repeated the same experiment 3 times with 3 other Influencers and similar things have happened.

They were sitting on a goldmine.

Chances are, you are sitting on the same goldmine too.

To me, social media was never about money.

It was about the challenge. (I'm a big believer in what Edumnd Hilary said,

"It's not the mountain we conquer but ourselves.")

I'd sold over $40 million online before I turned 30 using mostly email marketing.

Then email slowly started to plunge and I had to diversify. (Being reliant on only one channel in your business is a bad idea, and it was my fault for putting myself and family in that position in the first place.)

I knew social media was big but I didn't know how it worked.

I wasted a lot of time those first 18 months on social media, obsessively experimenting with every marketing strategy I knew or could find.

I wanted to go back to focusing solely on email marketing because I was so comfortable there but I had no choice.

And I'd become hooked on this challenge of "decoding" social media too.

Since then, a lot of money's been made but more importantly, I've had so much fun figuring out social media, figuring out this engine for Influencer Income and sharing it with others (and now you).

You and I are about to start an epic journey together.

Let's begin.

2 INFLUENCER INCOME

Before we begin, I'd like to tell you an odd but true story about the "Influencer Engine" for driving more *Influencer Income*.

When I was a senior in college, I had a run-in with my professor that made my blood boil.

In front of my friends, she said, "Jason, you're acting like a screw-up. You need to figure out what you want to do with your life."

I told her, "I have no idea what I want to do. But I know what I don't want. I don't want to spend my life working for someone else. I don't want to give away 40 hours of my life every week for a paycheck. I don't want to spend my life trapped in a cubicle surrounded by lifeless co-workers who look like they've had their soul sucked out. I will not settle in my life, even if everyone else is."

She must've thought I was delusional because she said, "Jason, you're a senior now. It's time to start being realistic. You're not going to be a pro athlete or a famous person. Do you think being a college professor was my dream? No. But it pays the bills. You're going to need to be smart and get a good job that can pay your bills too."

My blood was boiling.

I told her, "You're wrong, I'm not going to settle for that."

She said, "It's not settling, it's being realistic. You'll see."

It hurt to know my own teacher didn't believe in me. That she would belittle me in front of my friends and not even care. I walked out of that room more stubborn than ever. There was no way I would end up stuck as someone's corporate slave. That life just wasn't for me.

Around that time, I'd heard online about a small group of entrepreneurs who made all their money on social media and the Internet.

I didn't know anything about making money online but they were having a big seminar in Washington DC that I could attend. The idea of going somewhere new, where I didn't know anyone, scared me.

What if I went there and found out they were all scammers or something? You never know with these Internet people, right?

But I couldn't let my professors predictions become my future. I needed a way to make money that didn't require a job, boss or rush-hour traffic. I took most of the money I'd saved (working as a basketball trainer), got myself a ticket and headed off into this new world of online and social media marketing.

On the first hour of the first day of the seminar, I bumped into a man named Craig Ballantyne.

Craig was already an online millionaire living the laptop life. He had homes in Toronto and Colorado, thousands of customers and a lifestyle most people dream of.

Craig asked about my story. He seemed actually interested.

I couldn't believe it.

I felt like Luke Skywalker, when Yoda first shows a little bit of interest in guiding Luke.

If Craig could somehow help show me the ropes, then maybe one day I could become an online millionaire too.

As I began to tell Craig my story, my phone rang. It was my mom. She wanted to make sure I was safe in Washington DC.

I told her, "Mom, I can't talk right now. This millionaire is talking to me and I think he might want to help me. I love you, I gotta go!"

I told Craig everything.

About my goals.

About my professor.

I had no idea how he would respond. What if he said, "Well, keep trucking young man, you'll figure it out," and went on his way?

But instead, Craig told me, "Jason, I'd like to help you. If I give you the plan, and I promise you it'll help you make money online, and if I even show you others like you who are doing it right now, will you take action on it?"

Immediately, I said, "Yes."

Craig said, "Great. Give me $1000 and I'll give you the plan. And if you don't make an ROI, I'll walk you through the plan again and again until you do. Do we have a deal?"

I didn't know what to say. $1000 was about all I had left. But something in me told me to accept the risk and bet on myself. I was reminded of an old saying: "Jump first, and trust the parachute will open." I jumped and made the investment.

Right after, Craig sat me down in the hotel lobby, grabbed a napkin and wrote a business plan on that napkin for me. He told me, "Just follow this short plan. People make money-making complicated. But when you know the plan, it can be really simple."

I went back to college with Craig's Napkin Plan but I was hesitant to implement it.

Part of it required me to make videos. I was no good on camera then. Plus I had no special camera equipment.

Another part of the plan called for an audience of people to market and sell to. I had no followers or fans back then. I worried, what if I put this out there and no one cares? Or what if I get haters or trolls?

And what will the people who know me personally say when they see me online, trying to do this? Will they call me names? Will they say it'll never work? Will they think of me as crazy?

Then I remembered a piece of advice a basketball coach had given me. He said:

"Jason, people will have opinions about everything in life, including you. They won't have put much thought into those opinions but they'll have them. Just remember "Source, not Story". It means don't listen to the story of their opinion but *look at the source* of who's sharing the opinion. If you wouldn't trade your life with theirs, don't trade your time for their opinion."

After that, I became an "action-taking machine" and followed the plan Craig gave me exactly.

Within a month, I'd gone from nothing to making $20,000 a month from my dorm room.

My parents were in shock. My friends wondered if I'd started selling drugs. I even took my first $20,000 check and bought an Audi convertible to drive around campus in. I'll never forget what happened next...

I drove my new convertible to class one day and parked in front.

Right as I get out, my professor parks next to me.

The one who told me I needed to "get a job and be realistic".

The look on her face was priceless when she saw me with my new convertible.

I dropped out of college after that.

That was 12 years ago and since then, I've kept myself busy.

Most people today know me because they read my book *Higher Status* or know I generated over $40 million online before I turned 30.

Others know me because they read my guest column in Forbes, or know I was recognized by the White House as a Top 100 Entrepreneur.

But if I'm to communicate my message clearly in this book (no easy feat for the author), the thing I really should be known *after this book* is what I share *in this book*.

Not because I'm so special but because the "social media recipe" being shared in the book is.

My team has taken to calling it the *Influencer Engine* and for good reason:

If you'll allow me to help you install the *Engine* into your business, it will drive you to the top of your industry.

There are 3 parts to the *Influencer Engine:*

Remember this: Credibility is an Influencer's currency.

If you don't have credibility, no one listens to you. You share content and you get crickets in return. Very few people, if anybody, will buy from you or your company.

If you do have it, amazing things happen. People can't get enough of you and your message. The audience chooses you over your opponents. You always seem to know what to say and post. And it won't even matter if you're not charismatic or good on camera yet. The Credibility Part of the *Engine* overcomes all that too.

The Real Truth About Becoming an Influencer

In case you think you're not an "Influencer" yet or don't have the credentials, please realize there is no Influencer Fairy who visits you in the middle of the night and leaves a note under your pillow, proclaiming, "You're an Influencer now!" Nor is there a degree you must get in order to be deemed a "real Influencer". All Influencers are self-selected. You simply decide to be one. Or you don't. It's up to you. So if you're not yet an Influencer (yet) but want to find your message and develop the skills to become a true leader.. if you want to share your message and make your will felt on the world.. and if you want to make this a career so you never have a job or boss again… make the decision now. And if you're still unsure, remember the most expensive decision is indecision.)

The second part is **Connection**.

Understand: In the Digital Age, connection is flypaper for followers.

Without it, your follower count is sad. The audience is skeptical of you.

And if you get a hater, you have no "true fans" who will stand up for you.

But with Connection, you attract new followers like bees to honey, even if you're starting with one follower. The audience will not be able to get enough of you. They will truly, deeply *care about you*. And you almost never have to "sell". All it takes is a simple "call to action" to light up the cash register. But most importantly, the Connection part of the *Engine* will make your content incredibly sticky to your audience. While other Influencers get no loyalty from their band of followers, your audience will get sucked in like a soap opera.

The third part is **Communication**.

This isn't your typical "how to communicate with your audience on social media" stuff.

Nor is it more of the same "what to post" advice.

In the **Communication** part, I'm going to walk you through the Chat Engines my team and I have been using with our own accounts and our Influencer partners to drive more revenue per follower than anyone on social media outside of Kylie Jenner. I'm not bragging here, I'm trying to alert you to the fact that, once again, even if you only have 1,000 followers right now, you are currently sitting on a goldmine. If you have a much bigger audience, you're sitting on the Taj Mahal of goldmines. (And if you have no followers, you only need to get a few before you can be sitting on a goldmine too.)

Please note: That "goldmine" you're sitting on grows in direct proportion to how well you implement the **Credibility** and **Connection** parts of the *Engine*. Failing to do so will undermine your monetization efforts and that "goldmine" you're sitting on will turn out to be only a few mere shekels.

You might be wondering why would I do this?

Why would I share all this?

I have three reasons, one of which you might not expect:

Reason #1: There is an abundance of crappy social media advice published every single day.

What's scary is this advice can "look" legit and easily deceive people. Often, the advice comes from so-called "experts" whose only claim to fame is the fact they publish advice on social media, not that they've actually done it themselves. There's a very good chance *you* have consumed this advice, trusted it's source and applied it to your social media, only to get average or below-average results. I'd like to help fix that, if I can.

Reason #2: My team and your team might be a good fit for each other.

As I mentioned in the Introduction, a close Influencer friend of mine recently asked me and my team to apply the Chat Engine to his business.

I was hesitant to partner with him on it but eventually agreed to an experiment.

Before this experiment, my buddy's Instagram made him about $5,000 a week.

In the first 7 days, our system drove an extra $54,000 in revenue.

By the end of the first month, it drove an extra $121,000.

My Influencer friend didn't have to accept sponsorship money.

He didn't have to "sell out" and promote products he didn't believe in.

He didn't "burn out" his audience (what we did actually created more goodwill with his audience).

And none of this competed with any other promotions he was already doing or wanted to do.

We simply sold *his own products for him* but we sold it using a chat selling system that took us 3 years to figure out (the Chat Engine), along with the Chat Engine software that's become required for bigger social media accounts to have (otherwise they risk leaving half, or more of total revenue on the table).

I've since realized I could do an experiment like this with a small number of Influencers who wanted to add $1,000,000 or more a year to their revenue without them having to lift a finger either.

My "selfish interest" in writing this book is maybe those existing Influencers read this book, get excited by the idea of adding $1,000,000 a year or more to their business without lifting a finger and the good ones send me an email at **Jason@HighStatus.com** with the word "Experiment" in the subject line (so I know what you're emailing about).

By the way, I am simply not smart enough to pick the best clients so I follow Warren Buffet's sage advice on the subject: "Work only with clients who you like and admire."

Reason #3: Before Hitler's time, my great-grandpa was a famous musician in Amsterdam.

He sang for Kings and Queens. He was gonna sing for the President one day.

Then Hitler came.

My Great-Grandpa, along with his wife… his 3 kids… his brother and sister… were exterminated.

The lone survivor was the man who one day would be my grandpa.

He fled to Detroit.

He was completely alone. He had no money. (And he had just lost everyone in his family.) He did his best but **I want to bring my family back to the top of the mountain. Honor. Respect. All that stuff.**

So today I'm on a mission to create 100 millionaire students. (I've given myself 3 years to do it.) My plan is to write a book about their success stories, and let the book inspire people everywhere to live a life of freedom and prosperity.

I've helped created 10 millionaire students in the first 6 months so far *without this book* so I hope one day soon many future millionaires will say this is the book that got them started. Needless to say, I've got my work cut out for me.

Now that you've got the key parts of the *Influencer Engine* for driving more Influencer Income, it's time to begin with the **Credibility** part of the *Engine*. Let's begin.

3 CREDIBILITY

Picture this.

You and I go to Hollywood Boulevard.

Right near the Walk of Fame.

Tourists everywhere.

I set a podium down on the street, stand on the podium and start teaching.

Preaching.

Sharing.

Just giving out all my best tips, tricks and lessons, at the top of my lungs.

How many people do you think stop and listen?

And of those that do stop and listen, how many do you think will take what I say seriously? Maybe even begin to apply it to their life?

Your answer is likely something like, "Jason, almost no one would stop and listen to you dropping knowledge in the middle of Hollywood Boulevard standing on a podium. And those that do stop would be stopping for entertainment."

You'd be right.

I'd have little to no influence because to everyone walking by, I'd lack credibility. We as humans like those that influence us to be credible. We have no preference for average.

Imagine if no one knew who Donald Trump was and he was speaking from the box? How many people would stop and really listen to him?

Or imagine no one knew who Oprah was? And she was speaking from the box? How many would stop and listen to her?

Credibility is an influencer's currency. The more you have of it, the more influence you have. And more influence equals more engagement, more sales, more impact.

In 2014, when I was still a dating coach, a friend and I did a marketing test. We knew a female "influencer" with 1.7 million followers, and paid her $400 to promote a post for us.

The post drove her followers to one of our opt-in pages, where we'd get the user's email address in exchange for a free report (and then we'd sell them a dating course via email marketing).

Her post drove 1,700 new opt-ins in 24 hours. We were getting email leads for less than $.25. I was pumped. Look at these numbers, how could we not make money?

Marketing Cost: $400

Leads: 1,700

Cost Per Lead: $.25

Price of course: $47

To make our $400 back, we only needed to sell 9 eBooks. And we now had 1,700 leads to sell the course too. What happened?

We spent two weeks emailing those leads, using every marketing technique we knew. *We couldn't make a single sale.* And this wasn't an untested offer. I was selling hundreds of copies of this $47 course everyday to other traffic sources. But all that traffic we got from this female influencer would not convert into sales.

Why?

Credibility.

This particular Influencer had no credibility to her audience.

Her entire Instagram page was mostly bikini's, boobs and her butt. That's what her audience wanted from her. And it got her followers. But she had no actual credibility to her followers and again, *credibility is an Influencer's currency.*

So even though she sent us 1,700 opt-ins, all of them came in super-skeptical. And my marketing could not overcome their skepticism. You could have given me any other traffic source at the time - cold Facebook traffic, banner traffic, affiliate traffic, whatever - and I would have made at least some conversions. But I could not do it with her traffic.

This is an issue a lot of Influencer's have today. We call them Influencer's but they lack actual influence. Their fans will like their photos and watch their videos but won't take their influence seriously. And so these Influencers can't successfully market or sell any of their own products. They have to settle for sponsorships, promoting tea, protein powder and other kinds of pills or potions.

Recently I got an email from one of my millionaire students, Paul Tancredi. He was trying to help another female influencer sell a new course. She had 3.3 million followers but almost none of those followers were buying her new course. (I can't share the exact numbers but they were pretty bad.) Paul asked me, "What would you do to help them sell more?"

I told him, "I'd wish her team good luck and forget about it. No one's buying the course because she has no credibility in her audience's eyes. She has credibility for being hot. Which is how she built her following. They're not gonna suddenly believe she's an expert in the course and buy that too, just because they like her boobs and butt."

Remember: Followers without credibility is fool's gold.

You don't need to be a pretty girl to be plagued with an audience that follows you but doesn't take you seriously. I've met dozens of other Influencers in different industries and I'd estimate most have this problem.

Most Influencers on social media lack credibility in their audience's eyes. They think having followers gives them credibility, and it does...but not much.

This is why my account can have 1/10th as many followers as someone else's yet generate 10X as much revenue. Same situation with my clients. Not some of them. All of them.

Think of it like this: If credibility is an Influencer's currency, how much credibility should you want? As much as possible, yes?

Personally, I want my account and my client's accounts and your account to have bulletproof credibility. I want the other players in your industry to hear about the numbers you're doing and go, "HOW? How is that even possible?"

They won't know how but you will: There's a formula driving all that credibility.

This formula won't make an expert out of an amateur. But it will leverage every last piece of credibility you have and make the absolute most out of it.

Nearly every Influencer I've worked with had stockpiles of credibility they weren't aware of. Or didn't realize made them credible. I'm betting you have an unused stockpile of credibility too. It's my goal in this Section to pull that out of you and help you apply it immediately to your content and audience so you're not just another Influencer but *someone who has actual influence with your audience.*

There're only 3 key things we need to focus on:

- The Triple AAA
- The 3 Legs of Belief
- The Credibility Twister

Think of these 3 things like ingredients to a recipe. And this is the recipe for true credibility with your audience. Let's cook it up.

4 THE TRIPLE AAA

When I moved to Puerto Rico last year, I sold my Bentley.

I traded in the Bentley for a Jeep Golf Cart instead.

I drive my golf cart all around my community in Puerto Rico – to the gym, to restaurants, even to the farmer's market on Sunday mornings. I love it.

Why am I telling you this?

Because that story…and that Jeep golf cart are an asset of mine.

My audience knows me for helping people replace rat-race life with laptop life. The people who follow me are the ones who want to live the laptop life too. What do you think they feel when they hear I moved to an exotic island, and traded in my stuffy Bentley for a fun and wild Jeep golf cart? They want to do the same thing! They want to stop trying to impress people with material items, get off the hamster wheel and move to a beautiful island too, free as a bird.

The fact that I have something they want gives me influence with them.

The fact that John Wooden won 10 NCAA basketball championships and is probably the best coach/leader of all-time gives him influence over me (because becoming an even better coach and leader is important to me).

But if you're a solopreneur, you don't have a team and you don't plan on ever having a team, John Wooden's track record is probably not an asset to you, and he's probably going to be less interesting and have less influence with you, than he is with me.

These are examples of Assets.

The Triple AAA stands for:

- Assets
- Advantages
- Associations

To remember it, I just call it "Hutto's Triangle" because my good friend and marketing genius Kevin Hutto opened my eyes to it. (Plus because "Hutto's Triangle" sounds cool, like the Bermuda Triangle but for marketing and influence.)

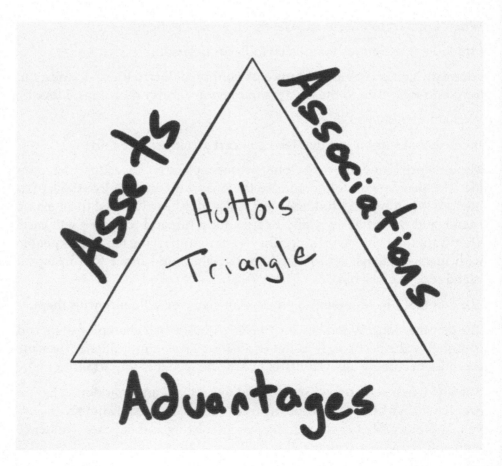

The Triple AAA is what gives you influence with your particular audience. We're going to build a list of each one, so let's define each of these ingredients first:

Assets are things you have that your audience aspires to have, or things you've done that your audience aspires to do too.

Advantages are the same as assets but they're also things that your competitors cannot claim, they are uniquely yours.

Associations are the people you're known to learn from, be seen with and teach.

I want you to imagine everyone of us keeps two types of folders in our brain.

One folder is red, one folder is green.

In the red folder is the list of names of people we would never buy from.

In the green folder is the list of names of people we *would* buy from.

Right now if your audience isn't engaging with you the way you want, or buying from you at the clip you want, you are in the red folder with too many people, and we need to get you in their green folder instead. The Triple AAA is the fastest shortcut I've ever seen to doing just that and making you the type of Influencer people like buying from.

ASSETS

Assets are things you have that your audience aspires to have, or things you've done that your audience aspires to do too.

This book started with Dan Bilzerian pointing a gun at me. Dan shows off his guns a lot on social media. Dan's audience aspires to have a lot of cool guns like Dan. Dan's guns are an Asset with his audience. If Dan decided tomorrow he was going to start teaching self-defense bootcamps, with former military badasses and real-live simulations, he'd sell out of spots right away, no matter the ticket price. When it comes to guns, Dan has credibility and they're an asset to his audience. Is this starting to make sense? I want you thinking about your audience and what would be an asset to them.

Let your brain begin to work on the answers...

What are the things your audience aspires to have?

What are the things your audience aspires to do?

Which of those things do you have?

Which of those things have you done?

Those are the things that go on your Asset List.

Remember that Assets are about the stuff your audience likes and wants.

Again, my audience is all about replacing rat-race life with laptop life. So while my Vladmir Kush painting might be an asset to me, my audience probably doesn't know who Vladmir Kush is. Most don't give a crap about it so it's not an Asset in this context.

I'll give you some examples of Assets that me and my team put together for my audience right now. Since Assets are about what your audience aspires to have or do, your assets should be somewhat different than mine.

I want you to notice too that not all of my Assets are expensive stuff. Sometimes, the best Assets are free, like a certain attitude you have that they want. Look at Logan Paul. His audience loves him, in part because they want to have more of that "maverick attitude" too.

JASON CAPITAL ASSET LIST

- Featured in Forbes, Entrepreneur, CNBC, Money Magazine (my audience wants to be known as smart, sharp, respected, etc)
- Best-selling author (my audience would love to be known as an author)
- Keynote Speaker (my audience wants to speak on stages to thousands of people)
- Wears expensive designer slides (my audience wants to be able to buy expensive things and wearing slides means you're not wearing a suit to work everyday)
- Jeep golf cart (as mentioned earlier)

- Relationship with Nataly (most of my audience is guys, and many would love to find an amazing girl to build their empire with)
- Defeated procrastination (huge sticking point with my audience, if I overcame procrastination, then I can help them do the same)
- Helped over 100 people replace rat-race life with laptop life in 2019 and helped create 10 millionaire students (these are case studies and testimonials, your audience will aspire to be one of them too)

My whole Asset List is longer but you get the idea.

Let's move on to your Advantage List.

Advantages

Advantages are the same as assets but they're also things that your competitors cannot claim. They are assets that are uniquely yours.

I'm a former college basketball player. That's cool. My audience would've wanted that. That makes it an Asset. But...none of my competitors played college basketball. That makes this Asset an Advantage for me. Does that make sense?

Often, the Advantages you'll have on your list will be things you would have never considered because you're so used to them. You don't think they're a big deal to your audience but they are.

A couple weeks ago, a buddy came to visit me and Nataly in Puerto Rico. We were deciding what to do for dinner the first night.

I said, *"Let's just get room service. The wagyu burger is insane."*

My friend said, *"Wait...you have ROOM SERVICE at your house? How is that even possible?"*

Immediately, I opened my Google Docs and added "Room service at his house" to my Advantages List. It never occurred to me to include the "room service" thing in my Assets or Advantages Lists, probably because I'd gotten so used to it, but to my buddy, this concept was a big-time Asset. And because none of my competitors can claim room service at their house, it's an Advantage for me in the marketplace.

Here are a few of the other things on my Advantages List to help you get going on yours:

- Recognized Top 100 Entrepreneur by The White House (my competitors can't say this)

- Former #1 Dating Coach for men (I used to hide this until I realized it wasn't a bad thing, it's something none of my competitors can claim and it gives me a very unique perspective)

- Sold over $40 million online before the age of 30 (I'm sure some of my competitors have done more but none are going to have the exact same numbers in the exact same time frame as me)

- Beach home in Puerto Rico, summer home in California

- Traveled to 25+ countries while simultaneously scaling teams and businesses (who doesn't want to travel like this? This one is hard as hell to do, by the way)

- Endorsed by Dr. David Buss, formerly of Harvard, and by former boxing world champion, Roy Jones Jr. (again, some of my competitors have great endorsements too but not from these two gems)

- The true story of my family being exterminated in the Holocaust and my mission today (this is my real motivation and my family's true story, no one else can copy it)

Are you starting to get ideas for what some of your Advantages will be?

And if you're reading this going, "Jason, I don't have any Advantages like these," I understand. Would you believe I thought I didn't have any Advantages either before I really thought about it? Then I realized Advantages don't just have to be about the peaks of success. They are anything that your audience aspires to and your competitors don't have.

For instance, what if you're just starting out and don't have any claims-to-fame? Well, what about the fact that you're the only one in your marketplace who's confident enough to admit they're just starting out? And so you turn that into an Advantage, by saying things like, "*I know nearly everyone in every industry fakes it 'til they make it. Well, I will never lie to you that way. I am just starting out building my online brand and I'm going to show you everything, including all the failures, all the challenges, all the setbacks."* Now your inexperience is an Advantage because your competitors aren't confident enough to say this and your audience aspires to be that confident themselves! Make sense?

Let's go to Associations.

Associations

Associations are the people you're known to learn from, be seen with and teach.

In The Prince, Niccolo Machiavelli states, *"The first method for estimating the intelligence of a ruler is to look at the men he has around him."*

We do the same thing today.

Your audience included.

When we want to know how legit someone else is, we (often unconsciously) first look to see who else things they're legit. And if it's enough people, or the right people, we assume they must be legit too. This is like social proof on a very macro level.

And I cannot tell you how many social media accounts I see where every picture and every video is just of the Influencer by themselves.

When we never see you with anyone else, we don't know if it's because you're choosing to do it that way, or if it's because in real life, no one's ever with you and you're not really the big deal that your follower count would have us believe. And it doesn't matter what the real reason is. If your audience always sees you only by yourself, you are missing out on a huge piece of the Credibility puzzle. Let's fix that right now with your Associations list.

You can think of your Associations list as being broken down into "Mentors, Peers, Students". We all have people we learn from, these are our mentors. We all have people we associate with, or do business with, or do hang out with, these are our peers. And we all have people we teach or mentor or advise, these are our students.

Your audience wants to see that you have all 3 of these.

Here are some of the people on my Associations list so you can start to create yours:

- Mentored by Dan Pena, Dan Kennedy, Ayn Rand, John Wooden, Robert Greene, Agora copywriters (notice how some of these mentors are people I've learned from in-person and some, like Ayn Rand, are people I've never met...they are my "virtual mentors", who are yours?)

- Seen often with Nataly, Bedros Keuilian, Sharran Srivatsaa, Kevin Hutto, Elliott Hulse, Brett Knutson, Alex Hormozi and my buddy Bryant (most of these are other industry experts or influencers but not all...your audience should know you have non-business friends too)

- Mentors or advises Kirby Robbins (my 1st Millionaire Student), Paul Tancredi (my 5th Millionaire Student), Andrew Wright (my 8th Millionaire Student)

Is this making sense for you? Do you know some of the people who will be on your Associations List right now?

For some reason, many Influencer's don't like admitting they've had mentors, or that they're currently learning from someone to their audience. They think it ruins their image. It doesn't. In fact, not sharing with your audience who you learn from ruins your image. Imagine if Moses came down from the mountain with the 10 Commandments and was like, "Yo guys, I just wrote this list of 10 rules for how we're gonna live our lives, let's all stop what we're doing so you can listen to me." Do you think anyone would have listened to him? But because he came down from the mountain with a list *from the big guy*, everyone was infinitely more receptive.

It's this weird bias we all have. When someone is sharing their own personal idea with us, we tend to meet it with judgement. But when they're sharing some other authority's idea, we tend to meet it with acceptance. The more you frame your lessons as coming from a mentor of yours, the more receptive your audience will be to it. Hiding where you got the information actually hurts you. So when making your Associations List, don't be afraid to pimp out your mentors or sources of insight. It actually gives you more influence.

Now you understand the Assets List, Advantages List and the Associations List.

And it's time for you to make your lists, if you haven't already.

Sometimes people ask me how many Assets or Advantages they should have? I tell them it doesn't matter. Think of as many as you can and put them on the list. When you think you've thought of everything, show your list to people who know you well (spouse, business partner, team members, close friends) and explain the drill to them. Ask them if there's anything missing from the list. They will think of things and see things you didn't because it's much easier to see the picture when you're not the frame. Add their suggestions to your list too, if it makes sense.

Now that you have your Triple AAA, it's time to dive into dive into the the 3 Legs of Belief and how a trip to Baltimore, Maryland actually taught me one of the greatest Influencer marketing secrets ever.

5 PROOF AND THE 3 LEGS OF BELIEF

Last year, I had the best steak of my life at the Ruth's Chris Steakhouse in Baltimore.

I wasn't expecting it.

We were hungry.

It was the closest restaurant nearby.

We sat down.

Ordered.

Then… it happened.

Best steak of my life.

I remember we all took pictures.

Not for social media.

But for ourselves.

To show our grandkids one day.

While I'm only half-kidding, that wasn't even the best part about that trip to Baltimore.

I'd been invited by Agora Financial, a $350 million dollar privately held publishing company, to speak to their massive marketing team, give them a few words of encouragement, then fly back to California.

After my little pep talk, I talked with Agora's head of marketing. He started to show me their playbook for generating over $1 Million a day online.

He said, *"There are no secrets. We out-sell all of our competitors because we have a knowledge advantage when it comes to marketing. They think Proof is important, we know it's most important."*

"What do you mean by Proof? Testimonials and stuff?"

"Proof runs so much deeper than just testimonials. Proof is anything that generates belief in the prospect. And without belief, nobody buys. Want me to walk you through everything? Take you down the million-dollar-a-day rabbit hole?"

I paused.

You ever have one of those moments when your gut is telling you, you're about to learn an idea that could transform your life and business, pay attention here?

My gut instinct was telling me that.

I called my assistant. Had her change my flight to the red-eye. I was staying in Baltimore for the rest of the day, ready to go down the "million-dollar-a-day rabbit hole".

The day was a blur as I filled my phone with pages of notes. In the Uber back to the airport, I remember the driver trying to talk to me but I could barely get the words out. My brain was fried, but my business was about to explode, thanks to the lessons I'd learned that day about Proof in marketing.

In today's Digital Age, our prospects see 5,000 ads a day.

That means by the time they're 18, they've literally seen millions of ads.

So have we.

How do we deal with this advertising onslaught? We decide "all ads are bullcrap" and do our best to ignore them.

Then, once in a while, an ad will hook our attention.

We won't really know *why* it hooked our attention, just that it did.

Wouldn't it be useful to know *how* those rare ads actually get you paying attention? Why do they work? How can you apply the same principles to your ads and your marketing?

As a result of 5,000 ads a day, we as a public now have trouble believing almost any message.

We don't believe advertisements.

We don't believe our politicians.

We don't believe our news.

We live in a world of empty promises.

And yet I learned at Agora that day that "without belief, nobody buys".

What's the solution?

Proof.

Proof generates belief.

Erases skepticism.

Augments the credibility of the message and the messenger (that's you).

I often think of the marketing environment we create with our audience like a garden.

Followers are like seeds.

And they won't bloom into a garden full of customers without nourishment.

Proof is that nourishment.

When we first started marketing my IG Agent training system, it sold well off the bat because it's a damn good offer and we had a lot of proof. A few of the students had made over $10,000 in the very first week. And these were students who had never made money in their life. One of them was still in high school.

But IG Agent didn't really take off until I decided to take this Proof lesson to heart. While visiting Las Vegas for a night at the Electronic Daisy Carnival (a mega music festival), I spent the day with my camera crew filming on the streets of Las Vegas..

Our goal was to find random, ordinary people on the street and teach them a part of my IG Agent System in just a few minutes.

Then, we would have them use the IG Agent System live on-camera, so viewers later on could watch these ordinary people make money on the spot.

At first, everyone on the Vegas streets were rejecting me.

No one wanted to be filmed.

I thought I was going to waste my entire day getting told "No" by strangers!

Then one guy said sure.

I showed him the system, he followed the script and in 20 minutes, he made $100 on the spot.

We filmed the whole thing, including me handing him the $100 bill he'd just made.

I was stoked.

We got a couple more people to give us a chance, and both of them made money on the spot too.

I hoped they weren't going to spend the instant cash they'd just made on booze or gambling but that was no longer my concern because we had recorded what Agora would call "the best Proof you can get".

It's called a Dramatic Demonstration.

This is where people get to watch the product in-action, producing the results promised.

With IG Agent, we promise if they can follow the steps, anyone can make money with Instagram. But instead of me just telling my audience this, we now had video proof of it, live from the wild streets of Las Vegas.

The day we put that "Las Vegas" video online, IG Agent sales went up.

They haven't stopped since.

Not only that but I had numerous Influencers reach out to me, intrigued by the IG Agent System, wondering if it could work the same wonders in their business. (Short answer is yes it can, but with a few key changes.)

Even the great Kevin Hutto reached out to me. He said the video was "the best marketing he'd seen online in 5 years".

For thousands of years, alchemists searched the globe for the Philosopher's Stone. They believed the Stone could turn basic metals into gold or silver.

While they never found the Stone for turning metal into gold, we have found the Stone for turning followers into dollars. It's called Proof.

And what if your goal isn't to monetize your audience?

Maybe you want to drive other actions, like donations for a non-profit, getting people to sign a petition, or compelling prospects to set an appointment? Proof is your Philosopher's Stone too.

Proof is literally social media "alchemy".

Take a look at this drawing here. We call it the 3 Legs of Belief.

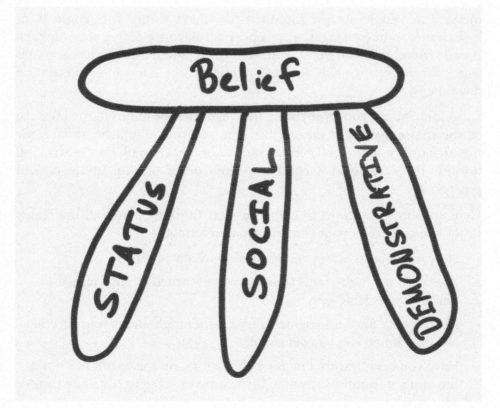

Now imagine a stool. How many legs does the stool need to stand sturdily?

You could probably get by with two legs but put 3 legs on a stool and you've got a stool that can stand strong.

Belief is no different.

There are 3 main "legs" of Proof I suggest you use almost exclusively:

- Status Proof
- Social Proof
- Demonstrative Proof

Status Proof

Status Proof is anything that increases the Status of the message, or the messenger. People are programmed to believe things that come from high-status sources. This is why Pepsi paid Beyonce $50 million dollars. If your friend tells you Pepsi is great and you should drink it, you might listen. But if Beyonce tells you, you're much more likely to start guzzling down Pepsi.

I also said Status Proof is anything that increases the Status of the message or the messenger. That means this type of Proof might be about your message or it might just be about you (or both). Overall, they're working towards the same goal: Generating more belief in your audience and prospects.

Here are some questions to help you start thinking about all the Status Proof you can use in your content and marketing:

- How many years have you been doing what you do?
- Are there any high-status sources you've learned from? Trained under? Done deals with?
- Do you have any endorsements from other high-status sources you can use? If not, can you get some?
- Have you been featured in any publications, online or offline? If not, can you get featured? (Even a tiny feature on a big website one time counts.)
- Do you charge higher fees than most of your competitors? (Higher

fees are actually a form of proof. To most people, the fact you charge more must mean you're better at what you do.)

- Do you "look the part"? In other words, are you a "fat doctor" encouraging your audience to lose weight? Or do you practice what you preach, and can you show your audience this?

- Do you have high-quality pictures of you? Maybe on stage? Or with high-status items (like nice cars, nice clothes, nice houses, nice views, etc)

Another really useful Status Proof technique for Influencers is getting your 3P Statement down pat.

The 3P Statement stands for "Person, Problem, Promise". It lets people know exactly what you do, who you help (and who you don't help). When done correctly, it can increase your Status in the marketplace significantly. For example, my 3P Statement is "I help ambitious people replace rat race life with laptop life".

Person: Ambitious People

Problem: Rat-Race

Promise: Laptop Life

Dale Carnegie was the author of the best-selling book *How To Win Friends and Influence People*. The book sold millions of copies its first few years in print, thanks to the strength of the advertisement selling the book. In that ad, Carnegie's 3P Statement was:

Dale Carnegie is the man the big men of business come to for practical instruction in getting along with people.

Person: Big Men of Business

Problem: Relationships

Promise: Practical instruction for getting along with people

What could your 3P Statement be?

Social Proof

Social Proof is the human tendency for people to think or behave in ways they see other people thinking or behaving. This summer, Nataly and I had just finished eating at my favorite sushi restaurant. As we walked out, we noticed a line of 25 people waiting at a gelato shop. I'd never noticed the gelato shop. Neither had Nataly. But now, with 25 people waiting in line for it, we noticed it. And I caught myself thinking, "If all these people are waiting for it, it must be epic gelato." That's the power of social proof. It's not rational but it's highly persuasive. (By the way, I did try the gelato later on and tasting it was almost a religious experience. In this case, there was a good reason for that place to have lines out the door.)

When people see other people trusting you, liking you, buying from you, it generates belief. Social proof works even better if the people they see doing business with you are like them (ie if I'm a college soccer player and all your customers appear to be grandma's over 70, I'm less likely to be influenced but if I were a grandma over 70 myself, I'd be highly influenced).

Here are some questions to get you started thinking about all the ways you can use Social Proof in your marketing and content:

- Have a lot of people done business with you? Do you have a lot of customers? Or a big audience? How can you promote that fact more?

- Do you have testimonials from customers or clients? If not, can you get some? And once you do that, can you get more? And if you already do have testimonials, can you get even more? (There is no limit to how many testimonials you can and should get.)

- Does your business lend itself to "before and after's"? Fitness is easy for this but most businesses could leverage powerful Social Proof by turning their customer's success into a "before and after" story with images, videos and storytelling.

- Have any publications featured your unique method? Your secret sauce? For example, I teach my students copywriting almost every week live in my Weekly Skills program. If Harvard Business Journal publishes an article about the ROI of copy, I'm going to use that article as Social Proof for learning copy. The article doesn't have to mention me for me to use it as Social Proof for copy. If you sell keto, and Netflix does a documentary on Keto, you should use that as Social Proof for your unique method (keto).

- Do any people of high-status follow you? Buy from you? How can you publicize or promote that more?
- Can you engineer your posts to get even more (real) comments?

I partied a lot in my 20's. When I think about Social Proof, I think about partying. You want to market your brand and business like your account, your website, your brand is the nightclub where "everyone" goes. (And you want to avoid any messaging that implies you're the club where no one goes.)

Finally, remember: People will always be more influenced by their friends than by marketers. If you tell them your product is the greatest thing ever, they probably won't believe you. You're expected to say that since it's yours. But if their friends are saying your product is greatest thing ever, they're much more likely to believe. How can you make this happen? Because I assure you, it's very likely if you have a competitor reading this right now, they will get what I just said too (about people being more influenced by their friends than marketers). But *they* will likely do nothing about it. That's just human tendency. Finding creative ways to generate more social proof, and the right type of social proof, will generate belief and move your audience to action in ways that almost nothing else can. I would conservatively attribute at least $10 million of my own products sold to the power of Social Proof. It is worth your time to make this happen. And get more of it in your brand and business. Rarely have I seen anyone use *too much* of it.

Demonstrative Proof

Demonstrative Proof is actively showing your product in-action. I had dinner last night with two marketers who spend upwards of $100,000 a day on marketing and advertising in their businesses. We all agreed a good *Demonstration* is the most powerful marketing tool you can own. It's ability to generate belief in your prospect is unparalleled. In every other type of Proof, you're *telling* them. With a Demonstration, you're showing them. As the legend of advertising himself Claude Hopkins said, "no sales argument can ever compete with a Demonstration".

You've seen Demonstrations before. Every good infomercial has one. In fact, most infomercial companies will not even consider marketing a product unless a *Dramatic Demonstration* can be used to sell it. A *Dramatic Demonstration* is the same thing as a Demonstration except the stakes are higher. If I walk across a rope 3 feet off the ground, that's a Demonstration. But if I walk across that same rope 300 feet off the ground, that's a *Dramatic Demonstration*. The stakes are higher. Death is unlikely in the first one, and only one misstep away in the second one.

I wish I could tell you what kind of Demonstration your product or brand needs but I'd have to know more about your product or service. The best I can do here is guide your attention to previous Demonstrations businesses have used successfully:

- Steve Jobs pulling the MacBook Air out of a manilla envelope on-stage during an Apple presentation (he was *demonstrating* how sleek and lightweight the Air was)

- The company behind the Blendtec (a badass blender) created a YouTube series called "Will It Blend?" as they put different items, like a Justin Bieber CD or an iPad, to see if the blender was strong enough to blend them (this is very much a *Dramatic Demonstration*)

- Nearly every good fitness or supplement marketing campaign will include "before and after's". "Before and after's" *are* a type of demonstration in that they actively show the results of your product in action

- When I went to Las Vegas and had people test my IG Agent System to see if they could make instant cash, that was a *Dramatic Demonstration* (because it could have failed and in fact, it did with a small percentage of people off the street - we include those "failures" in our marketing too to build even more belief)

- When Joe Sugarman hit the streets of Venice in the 1980's with his blu-blocker sunglasses and had people test them out then give their instant reaction, that was a Demonstration (you can find this on YouTube)

- More recently, a soap company called Dr. Squatch made a video modeling the Joe Sugarman Blu-Blocker Demonstration. With Dr. Squatch, they had people on the street smell their soap and give their instant reaction

- When a shirtless fitness influencer posts a video or picture of them eating ice cream or French fries, that is a Demonstration (they're demonstrating the power of the their product ie its so good, I can eat ice cream and still be shredded)

The key with a good Demonstration is the drama and uncertainty. The more dramatic you can make your demonstrations, the better. You make it more dramatic by raising the stakes. Will it work? Will it not? What are the consequences if it doesn't work? How can you heighten those potential consequences even more?

Remember, walking the tightrope 3 feet off the ground is a cool party trick. Doing it 300 feet off the ground creates true believers.

You now know your greatest barrier to more sales and more customers as an Influencer is belief. Our audiences have been trained not to believe anymore, thanks to a lifetime of commercials and the never-ending onslaught of ads they see everyday. And you know the cure to generating more belief: Proof.

You now have the 3 Legs of Belief, and all the different ways they can and should be applied to your brand and marketing today.

In the next chapter, I'm going to walk you through the system we use with our Influencer clients to make injecting all this Proof and Credibility into their marketing and content a cinch.

Let's do it.

More on The Power of Proof...

Recently I gave a talk at Fit Body Bootcamp Headquarters to nearly 100 of their franchise owners about the power of proof and how to apply it to their online marketing. I'd like you to watch this talk as well and make a study of the methods shared to be applied to your marketing. Go to **JasonsFitBodyTalk.com** to watch the entire talk now.

6 THE CREDIBILITY TWISTER

Imagine you're invited to a dinner party.

The host tells you, "You're in charge of dessert, and everyone at this dinner party loves carrot cake."

You go grocery shopping the day of the dinner party. You're looking at carrot cakes when it dawns on you. Sure, carrot cake is good. But strawberry shortcake is even better. Everyone knows that. Besides, it's your favorite and everyone at the dinner party will be stoked to discover an even better dessert than carrot cake.

So you skip the carrot cake and bring strawberry shortcake to the party. When it comes time for dessert, everyone at the party's ready to go. You bring out strawberry shortcake. Everyone looks disappointed. The host turns to a friend, "Remind me to never put a selfish bastard in charge of dessert again."

Here's our problem (and our opportunity):

We just spent two chapters going deep into embedding your content with seeds of credibility and influence. And we know credibility matters. A lot. It is an Influencer's currency, and you can't have too much of it in your content. But..

If we only put *what we want* in our content, we're ignoring what our audience wants. We're bringing strawberry shortcake to a carrot cake party. And we know how that turns out.

What, then, to do?

Allow me to guide you through the solution in this chapter.

We're going to take a deep dive into the Credibility Twister which has become a literal *dream come true* for me because it automatically injects Proof and Triple AAA into your content *and* it forces your content to "bring carrot cake to a carrot cake party".

That means your audience will eat it up. (Nom nom nom.)

To deliver our Credibility Content, we'll be using four simple tools:

1. The Credibility Twister
2. Water Temperature
3. Four Forces (a magical concept I learned from Taki Moore)
4. Siren Call's

A mentor once told me "success occurs at the margins." The world's fastest sprinter beats an ordinary runner by just hundredths of a second. In the social media game, you can beat your opponents (and enjoy the reputation of being the industry leader) by knowing your audience marginally better than anyone else does.

All we need to know is:

- Who is our audience? (at their core, not their shallow)
- Who's already influencing them? What's already grabbing their attention?
- What are their Four Forces?
- What matters most to them right now?

Once we know the answers to these questions, creating content better than their favorite dessert can happen automatically with the Credibility Twister (while most of your competition is still bumming everybody out with their strawberry shortcake shenanigans).

There are 3 key principles driving the Credibility Twister. Let's dive in:

Don't Bring Strawberry Shortcake to A Carrot Cake Party

Can I go deeper into this for a second? It's too important and too many Influencers don't understand it on the level they should.

There was a fisherman in Long Island.

Best fisherman the island had ever seen.

The local newspaper did a story on him.

Asked him, "How is it you're able to catch more fish in a day than dozens of fishermen will catch in a month?"

His answer has become one of the most repeated sayings within my team:

"I out-fish everyone else because they think like fishermen, I think like a fish.

When the others want to catch more fish, they go to the store and check out all the latest fishing gadgets. That's thinking like a Fisherman.

I go where the fish are.

I study them.

I see what bait they like, what bait they don't like.

What time of day they seem to be the hungriest.

I know more about the fish than they do themselves.

I think like a fish."

We must commit to doing the same with our audience and our content.

If we don't, we're at risk of first losing our audience's attention to an opponent who's thinking more like the fish.

But if we do, we not only hook in our audience much harder but our opponent's fish start to swim our way too.

What Matters Most To Them Now?

The great copywriter Robert Collier taught us we want to "enter the conversion going on in our prospect's mind".

It means we want to create or circulate content related to *what's already going on* in our prospect's mind.

It means we don't have to reinvent the wheel.

It means if we can just talk about the stuff our audience is already thinking about or talking about -- the stuff that matters to them today -- they will gravitate towards us like moths to a flame.

Dan Kennedy talks about the classic sales story involving the hot-shot salesmen pitching a new home heating system to a little old lady.

The salesmen tells her everything there was to tell about BTU's, construction, warranties, service, etc. When he finally shut up, she said, "I have just one question — will this thing keep a little old lady warm?"

We do this by listening to our audience.

By studying the fish's behavior.

Think: We spend so much time trying to guess what our audience wants. Why not just ask them? Or study what they already want?

John D. Rockefeller, one of the wealthiest men in recorded history, said, "Weak men have loose tongues. Success comes from keeping the ears open and mouth closed."

Obviously, brands and Influencers need to keep their mouths open, sharing their message. But Rockefeller was spot-on in encouraging us to take ourselves out of the equation and listening more to our prospects and audience.

We must address their priorities, not ours.

Demonstration Over Presentation

Whenever my team records a "talking head" video of me, I get worried.

I'm convinced that "talking head" video will not do well on social.

I'm convinced the watch rate will be low.

I'm not being pessimistic.

I've seen the data, with my own accounts and that of my clients.

I get to see what millions and millions of followers across almost every industry like and don't like, in terms of what they're visually seeing on the screen.

Here's what I've seen:

If the video is "talking head", which just means your pretty face talking to the camera, the video has a much lower chance of going "viral" than if it includes video of you (or others) actually *doing something*.

We talked earlier about the power of Demonstrations in the chapter on Proof, and I'm talking about it here again.

The more you can *show* instead of *tell*, the higher your watch rate will likely be.

Now that you know the key principles driving that'll be driving your Credibility Content, let's cover the simple tools you'll be using.

NOTE: I use these tools internally. We use them with our Influencer clients. They are magic. I can't imagine doing any kind of work on social media without them. Failing to do so will undermine all your other social media efforts.

We'll start with:

1. The Four Forces
2. Water Temperature
3. Siren Call's

And then we'll put it all together for you with..

4. The Credibility Twister

The Four Forces

If you've ever studied direct-response marketing, you've no doubt heard that you want to market to your prospect's *pre-existing* desires, dreams, fears, frustrations, aspirations and more. It's great advice but how do you really do that? Enter the Four Forces.

(I learned this visual tool from Taki Moore and have been using it ever since.)

If you think about it, your prospect's "fears" and "frustrations" also have what in common? They're both things your prospect wants to *move away from*.

And that means your prospect's desires and aspirations are both things your prospect wants to *move towards*.

If we know these two things, we have a blueprint for what's going to influence your prospect. Show them how your product or service move them away from what they don't want *and* moves them towards what they do want, and they're hooked *because it's what they already wanted and were hoping for.*

This is the first half of the Four Forces:

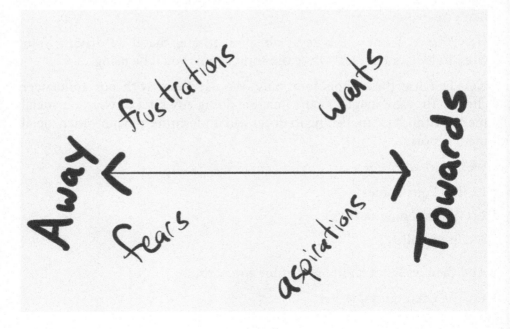

We also know the things that your prospect consider "frustrations" are things that are happening *right now* in their life or business. And the the things your prospect "desires", he or she wants *right now* in their life or business.

On the flip, it's not hard to recognize the things your prospect "fears" are things they imagine (FEAR = false expectations appearing real). Same goes for their aspirations (aspirations = a hope or ambition of achieving something).

Put it all together and you get the Four Forces.

Look at drawing below:

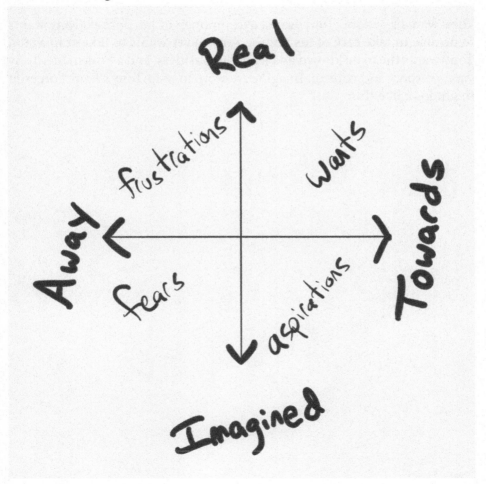

In the upper-left quadrant, you put the frustrations your prospect is dealing with today.

In the bottom-left quadrant, you put the things your prospect fears could happen to them if their frustrations continue to get worse and are left unsolved.

In the upper-right quadrant, you put the desires your prospect wants now.

And in the bottom-right quadrant, you put the aspirations your prospects hopes one day to achieve and experience.

For example, one of my main prospects is the guy or girl stuck in the rat-race and they want out. Let's call him Tony.

Tony wants freedom. Tony wants extra money in his pocket. Tony wants to be able to take care of his family. Tony never wants to take crap again. Tony wants the to be known as a leader in business, and a boss in life. Tony wants respect and control. Imagine we were to map Tony's Four Forces, it might look like this:

[98] Ibid., 154-155.

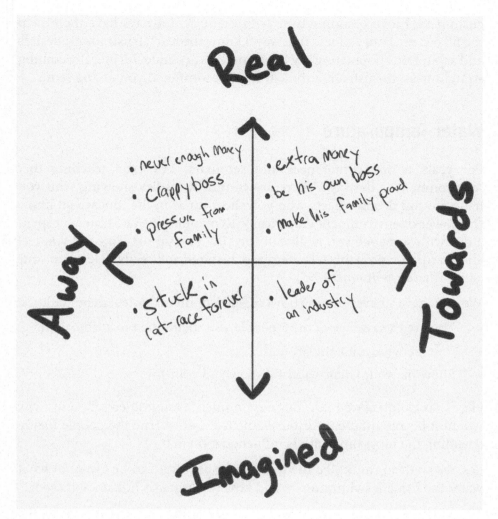

Your mission is to create a Four Forces for your prospect and then let it guide your messaging and your marketing. Keep it nearby you anytime you're working. It'll ensure you're bringing carrot cake to the carrot cake party and it'll keep you talking about the things that matter most to your prospect right now.

Quick tip: If you're sitting in a room by yourself and filling out the Four Forces for your prospect, are you thinking like the fish or a fisherman? A fisherman. We need you to think like the fish. Don't be the "All By Myself Entrepreneur" when you do this. *I love my audience.* I love my customers. I love spending time with them. So I always have them help me fill out my Four Forces. That way, I know the fears, frustrations, desires and aspirations populating my Four Forces is accurate. It's literally coming straight from the fish's mouth. I strongly recommend you do the same.

Water Temperature

For years at my conferences and seminars, I've been teaching that "environment is destiny". There are countless studies showing who you hang around deeply affects who you show up as in life. But we all know the power of environment empirically. Remember the last time you spent a day with someone you really admire and look up to? How did you feel afterward? You probably felt energized, inspired and ready to level up your game. That's *environment*.

We even have a never-ending bowl of "environment quotes" in our culture:

- "You are the average of the 5 people you spend the most time with."
- "You are who you hang around."
- "Show me your friends and I'll show you your future."

Here's my point: If we know our environment is so influential on us, why would it be any different for our audience? Isn't it true the people *they're* spending the most time with is influencing them too?

Yes, we want to think like the fish but we also want to be aware of what water the fish are swimming in, and how that water is influencing them.

That's why we call this tool "Water Temperature" because it "checks the temperature of the water our fish are swimming in" so we can know how that water is influencing them. It's really simple too.

We just want to know *what the environment is teaching and telling our fish.*

We break it down into 5 categories:

Teachers/School:

Gurus:

Books:

Blogs:

Friends/Family:

And we ask two simple questions for each category:

1. What are the most important things this part of their environment taught them?

2. What are the most important things this part of their environment is teaching them now?

For example, let's continue on with my avatar Tony and check the Water Temperature of the "Gurus" in his environment.

1. What are the most important things Gurus have taught Tony?

    - You need to set goals

    - You need multiple streams of income

    - Real estate is the best investment

    - Passive income is the best income

    - It takes money to make money

There's more but that's a good start. These are all key lessons Tony has heard over and over, probably for years fro Gurus and Teachers.

2. What are the most important things Gurus are teaching Tony now?

    - You should start a social media marketing agency

    - You need a funnel

    - You should do Amazon FBA

    - You need high-income skills

    - You need to stop hanging out with losers

It's not a complete list but you get the picture.

Your mission is to answer these questions for each of the 5 Categories (Teachers/School, Gurus, Books, Blogs, Friends/Family). And don't make the mistake of being the "All By Myself Entrepreneur" again when you complete this. Involve your audience. Include your top customers. Ask them to help you answer these questions. Think like the fish, not the fisherman.

Siren Calls

In Homer's *Odyssey*, Odysseus and his men are sailing near the Sirens. Odysseus knew that if a man heard the Siren call, he could not resist it. So Odysseus had all of his men plug their ears with beeswax and then, tie him to the mast of the ship. He ordered his men to leave him tied to the mast, no matter how much he would beg to be cut loose and go to the Sirens.

Siren Calls are the few, key topics your audience cares most about *right now*. I've found that if you identity these key topics, they will call to your audience like the Sirens did to men. Your audience will find them irresistible.

But we have to remember with our brand and content, we are not marketing to a statue. We are marketing to a moving parade. What is a Siren Call today may not be tomorrow.

One of the Siren Calls that my avatar, Tony, found irresistible for a while was Procrastination or Laziness. Anytime I released content including this topic, our views and engagement would go thru the roof. But now, that Siren Call doesn't do as well. I need to find out "what are the Siren Calls for my prospect right now?" just like you do. And then both of us need to design our content around those key topics.

Here are some of the best ways I've found to help you discover what your prospect's Siren Calls are:

- **MEDIA**. Look at the media, what's big in the news is probably something your prospect is thinking about too

- **SURVEYS**. Use surveys. Ask your audience what their biggest frustrations are right now, or what they're most curious about, or what they want most in life.

- **AUDIT**. Audit the comments sections. A lot of people avoid the Comments section because there's almost always some negativity or hate. I try to read all the Comments. Why would someone's negative comment affect my opinion of me more than who I'm showing up as everyday in my own life? So I don't avoid negative comments, it's just someone else expressing what they felt they needed to express in their own space. But in the Comments, the fish are basically telling you exactly what they were thinking and that's very *useful*.

- **STUDY**. Study your competitor's highest-engaged content for insights on what might be Siren Calls to your marketplace.

- **ADS**. If you have some experience buying ads, you can test a bunch of different possible Siren Calls and find which ones get the highest click-thru rate. For example, my team and I could ideate 20 different topics we think could be Siren's call to our audience. Then we could take a piece of content and give it 20 different headlines (one headline for each topic). Then we could drive $10 of traffic (using Facebook ads) for each piece of content and see which topics get the highest click-thru rate. It would cost us $200 to find the top 3-5 Siren Calls as well as identifying certain topics our audience doesn't care about at all right now. No reason you couldn't do the same.

Overall, you want 3-5 Siren Calls that you hit over and over in your content and brand until they stop working as much. Then it's time for you to do more research and identify what the new Siren Calls are going to be for your audience.

Also, often, the best Siren Calls are problem-based rather than solution-based. In other words, they're often about the things your prospect wants to move away from rather than what they want to *move towards*. If I talk about laziness, I'm talking about something they want to move away from. If I talk about having more energy, I'm talking about something they want to move towards. In my experience, the laziness angle will drive more views and engagement than the energy angle.

Remember: Problems grab more eyeballs than promises. I'm a super-positive person, so I don't like my content to always be about the things my audience wants to move away from but it does seem to work better.

Now let's take what we've just done…

1. The Four Forces
2. Water Temperature
3. Siren Calls

And put it all together with…

4. The Credibility Twister

The Credibility Twister

Have you ever noticed there are certain *types of content* that people are drawn to?

For instance, the Internet is littered with articles like "4 Foods To Never Eat Before Bed" Or "5 Things Wrong With Avenger's Endgame". These are Lists. People like lists. They're curious about them and click on them constantly. We know that Lists are a winning type of content but there are others. I've found these types of content to work best in every industry:

- Lists
- Q & A (answering an audience member's question)
- Case Studies (breaking down how someone achieved a specific result, could be a case study of something you did yourself too)
- Myth (bust a myth in your industry)
- Celebrities (celebrities get clicks)
- Rants (people like the strong emotions and authenticity expressed in a rant and are drawn to it)
- Tools (give people a done-for-you something)

In the Credibility Twister, we're going to combine these winning types of content with the Sirens Call you identified before to create content your audience will eat up *and* put you in a position of influence.

Let's say that we identified Tony's top 3 Siren Calls, and they were:

1. Laziness
2. How to make money with social media
3. High-Income Skills

This is what the Credibility Twister for my audience (ie Tony) would look like:

	Laziness	How to Make $$ with social media	High-Income Skills
Lists			
Q&A			
Case Study			
Myth			
Celebs			
Rant			
Tool			

On the left side are the winning types of content.

Across the top are the Sirens Calls.

All we're going to do is pick a Siren Call and a type of content, and it'll lead us to the winning content idea.

For example, let's say we chose Laziness (as the Siren Call) and List as the content type.

*What's a **list** about **laziness** that our fish might bite?*

Easy.

We could do, "3 Keys To Overcoming Your Laziness".

Or "3 Reasons You Feel So Lazy".

Or "6 Ways To Beat Laziness In The Morning".

Thinking up content ideas used to be so hard for me. And we'd go off the rails too much, creating content like a fisherman instead of thinking like the fish.

With the Credibility Twister, it's become easy. And it forces us to think like the fish because of the Siren Calls.

I look over the Four Forces before creating content to remind me of what life is like for my fish. It reminds me to address their priorities, not mine. Same thing with the Water Temperature.

But this is Credibility Content, right? Where does the Triple AAA and Proof come in?

Simple.

All we do is select a piece of Proof, or a couple things from your Triple AAA list and we ensure they get mentioned or included in the content.

For instance, one of my *Advantages* was I sold over $40 million online before the age of 30. So if I was creating content called "6 Ways To Beat Laziness In The Morning", I'd just make sure to mention somewhere in there my *Advantage*.

I could say, "Now after I learned this next way to beat laziness, I really started getting productive and I don't think I would have been able to sell $40 million online before the age of 30 without it, here it is…".

You want to do this with *every piece of Credibility Content you create*.

Now you're guaranteed to be sharing content that your current fish will find irresistible and make the other fish in your marketplace swim over to you.

And you're guaranteed to have the things that drive up your Credibility and Influence embedded inside every piece of content too.

Plus, none of it's hard to "come up with" anymore because of the Credibility

Twister.

Like I said, this framework has become a literal dream come true for me, and I hope it'll be the same for you too.

7 CONNECTION

"*My reach is down.*"

"*No one sees my posts anymore.*"

"*Where have my followers gone?*"

These are a tiny handful of the issues I've been hearing from influencers and brands for nearly a year.

Internally, my team's calling it the "Great Influencer Meltdown".

Organic reach is down.

The way you monetize *isn't* working like it used to.

And not to be all bad news bears but this *isn't* going to get better.

It's only going to get tougher, more competitive and more costly from here on out.. but it won't be that way for everyone.

How can you avoid getting scorched in the Meltdown?

First, let's just accept this is how *all* the major social platforms work.

At first, the platform wants you creating and sharing as much as possible.

The more good content you create, the more they reward you with reach and growth.

But eventually, the "money switch" gets flipped.

And the platform changes it tune.

Creating good content isn't enough anymore.

They change the rules but don't tell you the rule changes.

Typically, you have to start paying for the reach that used to be free.

If you don't want to pay, that's OK - the time, sweat and tears you put into helping make the platform such a stunning success has now brought them a silver platter of advertisers, ready to spend, at the demise of your brand.. your followers.. and your account.

Facebook was first.

Now it's Instagram.

Soon it'll be LinkedIn.

What are you supposed to do?

Let me tell you something about me I probably shouldn't.

Something my team wouldn't want me telling you.

Something that, in theory, should hurt my own credibility..

But my reach was down too.

Even worse, my story views were way down. (And I love Instagram Story's because they're a big part of the Chat Engines that drive so much revenue for Influencers).

Since my story views were down, so was my revenue.

I knew that Instagram's new rules were hurting my reach and everyone else's but.. I knew there was a way to figure it out too.

I have a saying my team hears me repeat a lot: "FOFA."

FOFA stands for "**Figure Out Fvcking Anything**".

I believe, if I commit to it, there is nothing I can't figure out.

I believe, if you commit to it, there is nothing you can't figure out.

There is no mountain too tall that FOFA can't scale.

My first attempt to reverse the damage was producing more content. Maybe if I just out-produced my competitors in sheer volume of content, the algorithm would reward me?

We spent 10-15 extra hours a week producing more content and made new hires to produce all the additional, new content. It did nothing. No effect on reach, views or growth.

My second attempt was blatantly bribing my audience to drive engagement up. We started giving random people $50 or $100 for "leaving the best comment" on a post, or just for watching my story's.

That helped a little bit (and still helps today) but it did not, and does not, produce the fireworks we're after.

There was a part of me that thought, if I just flashed wealth like some top influencers do (like with Lambo's, private jets, and Louie Vuitton luggage), that would do the trick.

But I'm just not into materialistic stuff.

I don't want to live my life doing things I don't like just so someone can give me attention.

For example, last year, I traded in my Bentley in for a Jeep golf cart.

I don't have a Lambo to show-off with, nor do I care to.

Besides, who knows if that would even work? My friends who flash wealth are still struggling as bad today as anyone else..

So basically, I was fvcking clueless and near the end of my rope when I sat down to dinner with my good friend and marketing genius Kevin Hutto…

(Kevin is so good at marketing, he's had days where he spent $100,000 on Google Adwords before breakfast.)

Over some damn good pizza, I told Kevin what was happening.

He paused for a moment.

Set his slice of pizza down.

Looked right through me.

"Jason, yes, views and reach are going down for all but they don't have to go down for you. There's another way."

"Dude.. I am to open anything right now."

"OK, here's your problem: You, like nearly every other influencer and brand out there, are all credibility and no connection. You need way more

CONNECTION. Your audience feels like they know everything they need to know about you when in fact they know almost nothing about you....

...you need to strategically humanize your brand. People will get sucked into it. I bet your views and reach won't go back to normal, I bet they'll go up. Way up."

"How do I humanize my brand? And my content?"

"I'll show you how I'd do it. Best part about this is most Influencers and brands will never figure it out."

Kevin spent the next 2 hours downloading everything into my brain.

The next morning I began to implement.

Within 24 hours, my story views doubled. (And with it, my Instagram revenue.)

I couldn't believe how fast it worked.

This happened overnight.

Don't promises of "overnight success" belong only on infomercials?

I immediately applied this new philosophy to my clients accounts. Same thing, same result. Their story views doubled. (And their revenue.)

Well, shit.

Winner winner, chicken dinner.

Several months later, my reach and views are riding stronger than ever. Same for my big clients. And we're thriving in this "organic reach recession".

In fact, a few weeks ago, my friend texted me in a frantic tone.

His story views had gone down 70% in a single day.

He said the same nightmare had happened for several of his influencer friends, did it happen to me too?

I checked my account and texted him:

"Nope. In fact, it looks like story views are even higher than normal for us right now."

As you start the next chapter, you're about to learn a secret most Influencers and brands will never discover. We call it the Flypaper Framework.

In the past I've been paid as much as $15,000 PER HOUR to teach this concept to an Influencer and his team. (I put "per hour" in ALL CAPS because being able to say you get that paid much blows my mind and the fact that it's me who gets paid that much just blows my mind even more. Beyond grateful. I still feel like I'm just a kid from Michigan who happens to really love all this marketing stuff and feels beyond lucky that I get paid to get even better at it every single day.)

Anyway.

As we enter into this next chapter together, remember this:

Connection *is* flypaper for followers.

I want my account, my client's account and your account to be sticky as hell. I want to make the fans and followers get glued to our account, to your account.

In the Digital Age, connection wins.

People are drowning in information but starving for connection.

We have followers, not friends.

If you can inject the Flypaper Framework I'm about to walk you through into your content and brand, you can protect your account and your business from the Great Influencer Meltdown that's already begun.

And I'm not just talking about surviving it, I'm talking about thriving.

You with me?

Then one little warning before we turn the page..

I tell this to every client..

If this is going to work for you, you're going to have to share some of the stuff you don't want to share with your audience.

Like personal stuff.

We call it "getting naked" with your audience. (My use of "getting naked" with your audience should not be confused with the influencers who've grown their accounts by *literally* taking their clothes off and getting just about naked.)

In fact, some of that stuff I'm going to ask you share may make your heart beat a bit faster.

This does not mean you should half-ass it. That's what 99% of brands and Influencers do and by doing so, they're choosing to be voluntary victims in the Great Influencer Meltdown.

Don't be like 99% of influencers and brands.

You're not a 99%'er.

You're a 1%er.

You wouldn't be here now if you weren't (and we both know it).

So please, do not enter into the Connection Section unless you're ready to "get naked" with your audience too.

Are you?

Great!

Let's do it.

8 THE CULTURE SHEET

I'm writing this to you on a Singapore Airline plane, waiting to fly to Thailand.

There are 8 total passengers here in first-class, including me.

Four of us are using a laptop.

All MacBook's.

Apple's got us hooked.

Apple's got a lot of people hooked. (They sold $260 billion worth of product in 2019. I'd say that's not bad.)

How does Apple do it?

Apple did something very different than it's opponents.

Apple didn't build a business, they built a culture.

People go into the Apple Store telling themselves they're buying a computer but really they're buying an identity.

An identity that says they're cool, hip and creative.

You want this with your audience.

People ask me how I sold over $40 million online before I turned 30.

I was a dating coach for men. (Like Hitch.) But there were a lot of dating coaches. How did I out-sell nearly all of them combined?

Because they were building a business, hoping a culture of raving fans would come out of it.

I set out to build a culture of raving fans, knowing a business would come out of it.

In this chapter, I'm going to teach you the Culture Sheet.

I have all of my clients use the Culture Sheet.

This past weekend, I built a Culture Sheet with one of our private Influencer clients. After, he said, "This basically covers everything you would need to create true raving fans online."

After I teach you the Culture Sheet too, I'm going to have you create your own.

The Culture Sheet is small enough to fit on a notecard yet powerful enough to generate millions of dollars in sales for any Influencer or brand online.

Here's what a finished version looks like:

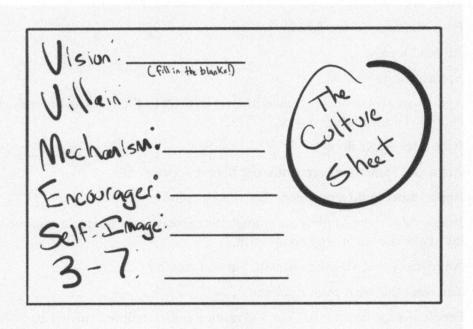

There are 6 components on the Culture Sheet:

- Vision

- Villain
- Mechanism
- Encourager
- Self-Image
- 3-7

That's it.

Let's go through each one right now:

Vision

Donald Trump created a big, triumphant Vision for the American people. He said, "We're going to make America great again. We're going to become winners again!"

Sometimes I ask people, what Vision did Hilary create for the American people? They have no idea what Vision Hilary created. Because she forgot to.

The influencers who make the most impact, and drive the most revenue, create a Vision for their audience to buy into.

You can think of Vision like heaven. You're offering a slice of "heaven on earth" for your audience, something for them to aspire to.

Here's my Vision for my audience:

I help people replace rat-race life with laptop life.

So to my audience, I am always talking about the PAINS of the rat-race and the PLEASURES of the laptop life.

They very quickly "get" that if I follow Jason, he's going to help me live a laptop life too.

The Vision for one of my clients is "making men strong again". He's offering his audience the chance to live a life of courage and strength, self-reliance and power.

What will your Vision be?

Villain

The best stories have the best villains.

Look at The Dark Knight. Christian Bale was great as Batman but Heath Ledger as the Joker made the Dark Knight one of the best movies ever.

There's Darth Vader in Star Wars. Thanos in Avengers.

But villains do more than make for great stories.

They bond us together.

Here's the takeaway: There's a villain standing between your audience and the Vision right now. You can (and should) use that villain as a powerful connection tool.

They did a study decades ago with kids at summer camp. They split the kids into two cabins, Cabin A and Cabin B. Then they had the two cabins compete against each other in various competitions. Very quickly, the two cabins started displaying hateful tendencies towards each other (amidst all the competition).

Then the researchers combined Cabin A and Cabin B, and pitted them against a new Cabin C in competition. Almost immediately, the heated rivalry of Cabin A and Cabin B cooled off. The same cabin members who were fighting the day before were now thick as thieves. What happened? The new, shared enemy (Cabin C) brought them together.

Your audience is no different. You want to make them feel more connected to you? Remind them more of the villain you both share.

The villain fighting against me and my audience is the rat-race.

The villain fighting against Democrats is Republicans (and vice-versa).

The villain fighting against a fat loss culture might be cravings, Monsanto, or the mainstream media which has created an impossible body image for you to live up to.

Who will your villain be?

Mechanism

The mechanism is the secret sauce that drives your audience to your Vision.

It's your method, your special formula to get results. It's not something everyone knows and uses. It's uniquely yours.

Think of P90X. What was their mechanism? Muscle confusion. They said things like, "The reason you haven't lost weight is your body adapts to the workouts you're doing and stops burning calories. The solution is Muscle Confusion, a breakthrough new exercise technique based on the latest science that keeps your body guessing and burning more calories than ever before."

It sounds good, right? (Ironically, "muscle confusion" wasn't a new breakthrough technique. Not all mechanisms need to be. P90X just took an "oldie but goodie" and renamed it. If your special formula to get your customer's results has been around for ages, just call it a new or different name like P90X did.)

When I sell IG Agent, my unique mechanism is the IG Agent Scripts. We show people how if they have the IG Agent Scripts, they can make money on social media. It's the "vehicle" that will drive them to the vision (laptop life).

What will your mechanism be?

Encourager

Every Presidential campaign employs a slogan. Something that will be repeated ad nauseam for months or years consecutively. Why? Because it works!

The repetition of the slogan gets ingrained into the prospect's head. Plus now you have your audience literally speaking the same language as you.

We call these slogans "encouragers" because we never want to forget that this statement needs to feel incredibly encouraging to your audience.

Think about the average day for the average person. The news makes it seem like the world is ending. Their coworkers smell bad. Hope is rare. And without hope, people perish.

So we lock-in on one Encourager and it becomes a symbol of hope for you and your audience, a constant reminder of what's possible for them.

My Encourager is Keep Fvcking Going. To drive this home, I had t-shirts made saying this slogan and I wear those shirts everyday now. I want my audience members to always keep fvcking going, to never give up either.

Russell Brunson, founder of ClickFunnels, uses "You're only one funnel away" as his Encourager. What's really clever is how Russell embedded his mechanism ("funnels") into his Encourager too.

Even Winston Churchill had one. He said, "Never, ever, ever, give up."

What will your Encourager be?

Self-Image

Self-image was a term made popular by the great personal development author Dr. Maxwell Maltz. It relates to identity. What kind of person are we? What are our strengths? Weaknesses? Limitations? Gifts?

But in creating a culture that acts as flypaper for followers, we're going to use self-image by answering the question, "Who does someone become when they *become* my follower or customer?"

This isn't an abstract concept, we want to come up with a name that everyone who's part of the culture will use to describe themselves as. Why? Because having a self-image that everyone in the culture shares creates a fence of deep-rooted connection for everyone inside of it.

Once you know the self-image for your culture, you'll be saying it all the time. And you'll know you're doing it well when your audience says it back to you. What are some examples?

My students become IG Agents when they sign-up with us.

When Apple ran those commercials "Are you an Apple or PC?", people started referring to themselves as an "Apple person".

My buddy Alex Hormozi sells to gym owners. When someone joins his program, they become a "Gym Lord".

If you follow Logan Paul, you're a "Maverick".

What will your self-image be for your culture?

3-7

I've been into self-education since I was 13 years old. My first purchase was Dale Carnegie's How To Win Friends and Influence People.

I remember reading it while on a plane with my family.

I read this great line in the book and wanted to share it with my Dad. I said, "Dad, did you know that if you want to be interesting, you should be.." and before I could finish the statement, my dad finished it for me.

He said, "..interested. If you want to be interesting, you should be interested. That's the old Dale Carnegie line."

"Dad, when's the last time you read this book?"

"I'm not sure. Probably 20 or 30 years ago."

I was amazed. How could an author create a saying that people would remember 20 or 30 years later? Or for the rest of their lives?

I've since figured out that the best teachers, gurus, leaders, CEO's and influencers have a set of key sayings that they say over and over and over. And typically, they have 3-7 sayings that get repeated most often.

These sayings represent what you believe are the key drivers of success, in whatever field they happen to be in.

Tony Robbins:

- Biography is not destiny
- It's in the moments of decision that our destiny is shaped
- If you can't, you must

John Wooden

- Make each day your masterpiece

- Drink deeply from good books
- Never mistake activity for achievement

Buddha:

- What we think we become
- There's only two mistakes one can make along the road to truth, not starting and not going all the way
- It is better to travel well than to arrive

You're smart. You know what it takes to get a result. But if you constantly describe that way with 1,001 sayings, you end up confusing your audience. And confused minds don't buy.

You want to lock-in one 3-7 key sayings that you'll repeat (yes, like a broken record) until your audience starts saying them for you.

What will your 3-7 be?

Now that you have the Culture for your brand and audience, it's time for the second ingredient in the Connection recipe -- Confessions.

9 THE CONFESSION WHEEL

Can love be controlled?

Dr. Arthur Aron, a researcher from Stony Brook University, set out to answer that question in his now infamous "36 Questions That Lead To Love" study.

In the study, participants would get into groups of two (one man, one woman) and ask each other a series of 36 questions, with the questions becoming increasingly personal.

Dr. Aron's idea was that "escalating reciprocity of vulnerability fosters closeness". In normal people terms, that means "as you share increasingly personal stuff with someone else, and they share increasingly personal stuff with you, a deep sense of closeness forms". Dr. Aron's questions were designed to do just that.

Did it work? Does the idea have legs?

Dr. Aron wrote, "The very first couple that pilot tested the questions were research assistants in our lab…they didn't know what this was about. They actually fell in love and got married, and invited the rest of the lab to their wedding."

Now instead of having you Google what Dr. Aron's 36 questions were, I'm re-printing them at the end of this chapter (when you go through them, notice how they start small and become increasingly personal as you go).

Dr. Aron's research is fascinating but what does it have to do with the connection you have with your audience? It turns out, a lot…

The key to Dr. Aron's research is self-disclosure.

Think of self-disclosure as sharing personal things about yourself (others might call it being vulnerable…it's not easy for most people to keep sharing personal things so Dr. Aron's questions helped force the self-disclosure out of them.)

Now where else do you think this idea of self-disclosure, and "escalating vulnerability" might come in handy?

If you guessed "with my audience", you get a gold star on your chart because you're right. The more you self-disclose to your audience, the stronger the connection they'll feel with you.

And we need that connection because in the next few years, we're going to see more and more people building powerful brands on social media.

Your competition is multiplying.

And you don't stand out with content, you stand out with connection.

People are drowning in content but starving for connection.

For example, look at the music industry. My girlfriend Nataly commented the other day that "nearly every one of Post Malone's songs are him crying over some ex-girlfriend".

It's true, Post Malone does have a lot of songs about ex-girlfriends. His pain. His hurt. His longing for them.

Now tell me this: Who else on this planet do you think can relate to thinking about their ex? Almost everybody. So as Post *discloses* and *confesses* more about his relationships with ex's, his fan base feels more and more connected to him.

This is why fans will obsess over Post Malone but not Rae Sremmurd. Post discloses and confesses more about his personal life, and he does it honestly.

Who has more die-hard fans, Eminem or T.I.? *Eminem.* Who has disclosed and confessed more through their content (ie music)? *Eminem.*

Self-disclosure is the key to fostering connection with your audience, in the music industry, celebrity industry, guru industry, and especially on social media. I call this kind of connection content that makes your audience binge your stuff and buy your offers "Confessions".

To make this kind of content pain-free for me, I use something called the Confession Wheel and I'm going to share it with you in a few moments. But first, let me give you the 3 keys to utilizing Confessions in your brand:

Fvck Perfect

A lot of brands and influencers are uncomfortable self-disclosing, or *confessing*, because they think they'll lose credibility with their audience. They believe their audience follows them because the audience believes they're perfect and disclosing imperfections would mean losing followers and fans.

This is, of course, preposterous. You're not perfect. Neither am I. And we also know no one else on Planet Earth is perfect. So if you're operating under the delusion your audience likes you because you or your life seems so perfect to them, step out from under it and join us in reality.

I'm going on Logan Paul's Impaulsive podcast in a few months.

Millions of people listen to the show so I want to be as prepared as possible. My goal is to give that audience the most value I can. I'm excited. But..

There's also "uncomfortable questions" I could get asked by Logan on the show. These are the questions I would prefer not to be asked. They're personal. They're controversial. And they'd definitely prove to the audience I'm not perfect.

Part of me still wishes we never had to talk about them but that's the whole point: Everyone's happy to talk about their strong points. But ask them about that failed product launch they swept under the rug, or that bad breakup they had with a partner, or their ongoing battle with food cravings, or depression, or the fact they have 350,000 followers but work at Urban Outfitters, or whatever it might be, and they're quiet as a mouse.

"You want me to talk about that? I don't want anyone to know about that, especially my audience!"

What these people fail to miss is this:

The more you share what you don't want to, the stronger the connection.

For example, here's a short list of what some of those questions I could get from Logan Paul on his show:

- Why do you live in Puerto Rico? Are you skipping out on taxes?
- Why don't you use your legal name in your business?
- You made millions when you used to be a dating coach. Did you teach guys to trick girls into bed?

You get the idea. I'm not even fully comfortable sharing these questions with you here…but it doesn't matter. Feel the discomfort, and act any way.

Remember: Share *more* of what you don't want to and they'll want more of you.

(By the way, to answer those questions above, I live in Puerto Rico because I love the island, I love the community I live in and yes, they have a much better, legal tax plan than the State of California where I used to live. I don't go by my legal name, which is Alex Maroko, because my first online business was called "Alex Maroko Basketball" and I sold it years ago. Because the buyer got the rights to continue using my legal name to market the basketball products, I didn't want to compete with my legal name in Google search. So I became Jason Capital in my next online business and it's stuck ever since. Today, 98% of people who know me call me Jason, including some family. And yes, I made millions as a dating coach teaching guys how to become the highest-status, and most honest, version of themselves. My tagline was literally "America's Honest Dating Coach". I taught then, and still believe now, that honesty is the best policy with the opposite sex. "Tricks" are for kids -- honesty is for adults.)

I've worked with over 1 million people in the last 12 years in over 100 countries. I've learned it doesn't matter where you're from or what industry you're in or who your audience is, we all have questions we don't want to be asked because then people will know we're not perfect, that we do have flaws. Do you know what I'm talking about here? If so, then you're sitting on a goldmine. That thing you'd rather not share but are thinking about right now, you know exactly what I'm talking about, is exactly the thing you need to be sharing more of with your audience. It is gold for fostering connection.

The magnificent thing is, the minute you start sharing some of your imperfections or flaws, your audience perks up and starts really engaging with you and your content. It's almost like they're bees and your flaws are honey. The flaws humanize you.

Plus by confessing your flaws, you get to put whatever spin on them you want. When I was in high school, I knew a kid named Nick. Nick had normal hair on top but this weird sideburn thing going on. His sideburns would grow super thick and they did this odd curl thing at the bottom. To this day, I've never seen anything like it. But more amazing was how Nick handled it. One day before class, two kids were trying to make fun of Nick's weird curl in front of some girls. But Nick just laughed and said, "Ohh, you're talking about the Love Curl? It's kind of epic, isn't it?" Just the way Nick said it and owned it - The Love Curl - made the other kids change their tune. "The Love Curl? That's genius, I guess it is pretty epic."

Fvck perfect.

Warts 'n All

This is no time for PhotoShop. The ideal is we're sharing all kinds of personal stuff with our audience, warts 'n all. And this is a tough ideal to swallow, especially for millennials.

Best-selling author Simon Sinek says that millennials filter themselves and their image on social media more than any other generation. He means millennials are great at making it look like their lives are like a glorious garden when in reality it's more like a bunch of weeds.

So I know the idea of *honestly* self-disclosing might make you uncomfortable. I know you'd love to continue on showing your audience only the best parts about you, your brand, your products, your life. But one, everyone is doing that so you won't be able to stand out. And two, you'd be leaving so much connection on the table...and for what? Because you're a little apprehensive to start really getting real and raw with your audience?

When you arrive to the Four Seasons Resort in Lanai (a private Hawaii island owned by billionaire Larry Ellison), you'll see an absolutely majestic garden of flowers overlooking the ocean. As you begin to take a closer look at each of these flowers, you'll notice *not a single flower is hiding any of its petals.*

Flowers don't have "good petals" and "bad petals". They open up completely.

You're not a flower but you are a beautiful, badass human being. Your petals make you who you are. Hide none of your petals. Share all of them with the world. Warts 'n all.

Content is Commodity, Characters Are Not

Content is everywhere. 300 hours of video are uploaded to YouTube every minute. Over 95 million posts are made to Instagram a day. There are millions of tips, lists, workouts, recipes and "secrets" available for free online. You can pay someone $5 on Fiverr to create decent content.

Millions of people produce content. Yet only a few thousand have developed a character their audience will stick to like flypaper. Would you rather complete with millions of people, or a few thousand? Content is a commodity. But Characters are a rare thing indeed.

When I say Character, I don't mean a role you play on social media. Character is the person your audience perceives you to be and how closely connected they feel to that person. We're going to use something called the Confession Wheel to make creating your Connection Content pain-free.

The Confession Wheel

My team has discovered there are 7 key areas we can (and should) get personal with our audience about.

They are:

- Business
- Health
- Travel

- Family
- Entertainment
- Food
- Personal

Putting it all together, the Confession Wheel looks like this, with each key area being one spoke of the wheel:

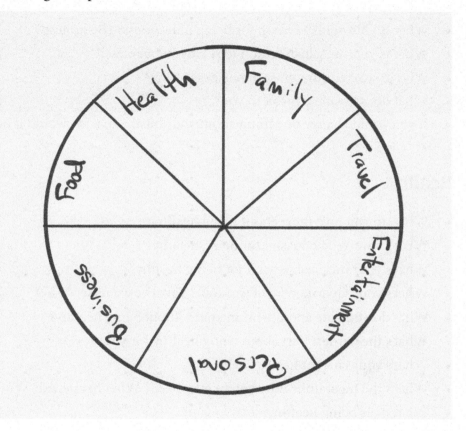

You want to be *confessing* and *self-disclosing* stuff from each of these categories on a regular basis with your audience.

What exactly should you be sharing? I've compiled a list of questions for each key area to get your brain going, your answers to these questions will foster a deep sense of closeness with your audience almost overnight...

Business

- What have been some of your biggest wins in business?
- What have been some of your biggest losses in business?
- What's the biggest struggle you've ever overcome in your business?
- What are you struggling with most in your business right now?
- What are you most excited about in your business right now?
- What is your selfish reason for being in business? (Be honest!)
- What is your unselfish reason for being in business?
- Who do you admire most in business? Why?
- What does business mean to you?
- If you could change one thing about your business, what would it be?

Health

- What do you love most about being healthy?
- What's your selfish reason for being healthy?
- What's your unselfish reason for being healthy?
- What's your favorite type of workout? Favorite exercise? Why?
- What do you hate about working out? About being healthy?
- What's the hardest part about being healthy for you?
- What's your current health goal?
- What's the most unhealthy you've ever been? What happened? Why?
- What does being healthy mean to you?
- Is anyone in your life unhealthy? How do you feel about that?

Travel

- What's the best trip you've ever taken?
- What's the worst trip you've ever taken?
- If a genie could grant you this wish, what would be your ideal dream vacation?
- What are the top 5 places you'd love to visit?
- What's your next trip? Why are you excited for it? Is there anything about it that worries you?
- What do you hate most about traveling? What do you love most about traveling?
- What does traveling mean to you?

Family

- Who do you love most in your family?
- Who loves you most in your family?
- Who in your family are you closest with?
- Who do you wish you were closer with in your family?
- Who in your family do you not get along with? Why?
- What's your most cherished memory with your dad? Your mom? Siblings? Grandparents?
- Why is family important to you?
- What does family mean to you?

Entertainment

- What music do you love? Who is your all-time favorite artist?
- What is your favorite TV show?
- What's your stance on watching TV in general?
- What's your favorite YouTube channel to watch?
- What's your favorite sports team? Who's your favorite player?
- What's the best movie you've ever seen?
- What do you like to do at night before bed?

Food

- What food do you find irresistible?
- What food do you hate?
- What food do you crave?
- What do you have a sweet tooth for? What food is your guilty pleasure?
- What popular food do you dislike?
- What's your relationship with food like?
- What's your favorite restaurant? What do you get there?
- If you were stranded on a deserted island and could bring only 3 foods with you, what would they be?

Personal

- What are you personally struggling with right now?
- What's your favorite thing to do in the whole wide world?
- In what way, if any, do you have a little bit of Imposter Syndrome?
- What's something about you only your best friend knows?
- What have been the 3 biggest regrets of your life?
- What have been the 3 biggest triumphs of your life?
- Do you have any weird or silly skills? Secret talents?
- What's the scariest thing you've ever done?
- Who do you love most? Who loves you most?
- What's something embarrassing about you that almost no one knows?
- What in your life do you feel most grateful for?
- What in your life do you feel most ashamed for?
- What in your life are you most excited about now?
- If you never had to work again, what would you do with your time?
- What's your biggest hobby outside of what your audience knows you for?
- What is most important in life?
- What's something you don't want your audience to know about you?

Now you have the recipe for creating a connection with your audience and making your brand as sticky as flypaper.

The first ingredient was Culture, the second Confessions.

Now it's time to combine these two ingredients and bake them right in to your content in the next chapter. Let's do it.

DR. ARON'S "36 QUESTIONS THAT CREATE LOVE"

1. Given the choice of anyone in the world, who would you want as a dinner guest?

2. Would you like to be famous? In what way?

3. Before making a phone call, do you ever rehearse what you're going to say? Why?

4. What would constitute a perfect day for you?

5. When did you last sing to yourself? To someone else?

6. If you were able to live to the age of 90 and retain either the mind or body of a 30-year old for the last 60 years of your life, which would you choose?

7. Do you have a secret hunch about how you will die?

8. Name three things you and your partner appear to have in common.

9. For what in your life do you feel most grateful?

10. If you could change anything about the way you were raised, what would it be?

11. Take four minutes and tell your partner your life story in as much detail as possible.

12. If you could wake up tomorrow having gained one quality or ability, what would it be?

13. If a crystal ball could tell you the truth about yourself, your life, the future or anything else, what would you want to know?

14. Is there something that you've dreamt of doing for a long time? Why haven't you done it?

15. What is the greatest accomplishment of your life?

16. What do you value most in a friendship?

17. What is your most treasured memory?

18. What is your most terrible memory?

19. If you knew that in one year you would die suddenly, would you change anything about the way you are now living? Why?

20. What does friendship mean to you?

21. What roles do love and affection play in your life?

22. Alternate sharing something you consider a positive characteristic of your partner. Share a total of five items.

23. How close and warm is your family? Do you feel your childhood was happier than most other people's?

24. How do you feel about your relationship with your mother?

25. Make three true "we" statements each. For instance, "we are both in this room feeling..."

26. Complete this sentence "I wish I had someone with whom I could share..."

27. If you were going to become a close friend with your partner, please share what would be important for him or her to know.

28. Tell your partner what you like about them. Be honest this time, saying things that you might not say to someone you've just met.

29. Share with your partner an embarrassing moment in your life.

30. When did you last cry in front of another person? By yourself?

31. Tell your partner something that you like about them already.

32. What, if anything, is too serious to be joked about?

33. If you were to die this evening with no opportunity to communicate with anyone, what would you most regret not having told someone? Why haven't you told them yet?

34. Your house, containing everything you own, catches fire. After saving your loved ones and pets you have time to safely make a final dash to save any one item. What would it be? Why?

35. Of all the people in your family, whose death would you find most disturbing? Why?

36. Share a personal problem and ask your partner's advice on how he or she might handle it. Also, ask your partner to reflect back to you how you seem to be feeling about the problem you have chosen.

10 THE CONNECTION TWISTER

I wish my mom never watched TV.

I really do.

Don't get it twisted: I love my mom. Love talking with her, love seeing her, love spending time with her. But even one hour of TV a day means your grave will say, "Here lies a great person who also spent 25,915 hours watching TV."

Growing up, my mom had a show she would watch every night. Usually, it was a reality TV show and that little detail means everything here.

I took my mom to dinner the first time she visited me at my place in Corona Del Mar, Orange County. We went to a place called The Quiet Woman. Why'd I take here there?

Because I knew, on one of the shows she watches, Real Housewives of Orange County, all those desperate housewives had dinner at The Quiet Woman and gotten into a raucous food fight there. I figured she'd get a kick out of eating there. And she did.   (Even crazier, the last person to live in my new house before I moved in was Shannon Beador, one of the "real housewives" of Orange County. You can go on People.com and see her giving a house tour of the place.)

Over dinner, my mom told me briefly about the show. She told me which "real housewife" was friendly and which one was a "total bitch". She said,

"I feel like I know all of them but I know it's so silly, it's just a TV show."

That.

That statement right there: "I feel like I know all of them."

That's the key for what we're doing with our audience.

And it's not just my mom.

More people watched the wedding of Prince Harry and Meghan Markle than any Super Bowl, ever.

People become addicted to certain characters they see on TV. I want to help you become one of those characters to your audience, not because it's good for your ego, but because it's good for business and the impact you're going to make.

And you won't need to be a Hollywood screen-writer or have a giant budget to make it happen. All you're going to need is a phone with a camera and the Connection Twister.

I'm assuming you have the phone+camera part, so in this chapter, I'm going to show you the Connection Twister. You'll see how it's going to make creating and sharing your Connection Content a breeze. With the Connection Twister, I could go on for 30 years and never run out of Connection Content ideas. And all of it would be sticky as hell to my audience like flypaper, same it'll be for you.

The only difference between us and those desperate housewives is there will be nutrition in our content, while theirs is only empty calories.

I know you're ready to get into the Connection Twister so no more waiting, let's dive right in.

Here is the Connection Twister in all its wonderful glory:

	Health	Travel	Business	Family	Entertainment	Food	Personal	
Reveals								
Demo's								
Just Happeneds								
Live Look-In								
Public Journaling								
Rants								

You should recognize the categories at the top. Those are the sections of the Confessions Flywheel we covered in the last chapter. Going down the left side are the different ways you can deliver the Connection Content to your audience. We'll call them "Content Delivery Types".

Reveals

The first Content Delivery Type is called "Reveals". In this type of content, you look straight at the camera and reluctantly share something you're not totally comfortable sharing. If you've ever seen the Jersey Shore, this is similar to when Snooki or the Situation would go into the Confessional Room and let it out.

Demo's

The second Content Delivery Type is called "Demos". In this type of content, you're going to actually be doing something instead of talking about it. For years, I've coached my clients and my team "Demonstration over Presentation". It means audiences will listen to you present but they'd rather watch you demonstrate. People would rather watch you do yoga, apply makeup or lift weights than just talk about it. When we combine you doing something with self-disclosure or confessions, we get connection hooked up to a tractor beam.

Just Happened's

The third Content Delivery Type is "Just Happened's". In this type of content, you're going to be responding to something that "just happened". Usually, it's in response to something a villain just did or an incident that just happened. A couple weeks ago, my dog Kennedy came into the house with a lizard's tail in his mouth. (He'd found one outside and did what dogs do to lizards.) I instantly made a "just happened" story, showing the audience what just happened and disclosed my honest opinion that there's literally nothing my dog could do that would make me mad at him. Note that these things don't literally need to have "just happened". If it's been a few hours, or even a few days, that's fine too.

Live Look-In

The fourth Content Delivery Type is called a "Live Look-In". In this type of content, you're going to share what you're up to or working on right now. You're giving the audience a "live look-in" to your life or work at this very moment. People love to see "how the sausage is made" and this type of content is ideal for showing them. Be sure to BE OPEN and share it all with them, warts n' all.

Public Journaling

The fifth Content Delivery Type is called "Public Journaling". Very few people have the courage to share this type of Connection Content but those that do find it tantalizing in its power because the connection can go so deep. Here, you're going to make an entry to your journal but you're going to do it publicly. Sometimes in my Instagram Stories, I'll post a block of text as my Public Journal. I'll type the words as if they were an entry into my personal journal but I'll share it publicly. The responses we get every time tell me I need to do even more of this.

Rants

The sixth and final Content Delivery Type is "Rants". You know what a rant is. That's what you're going to do here. This isn't you publicly complaining but getting something off your chest, like good friends do with each other.

Now that you know the 6 Content Delivery Types for Connection Content, let's put it all together using the Connection Twister.

I want you to pick one category on the left side of the Twister, and one on the top.

Let's say you chose "Reveals" on the left side, and "Family" from the categories on top. Great. Here's how it works:

You're going to answer one of the "Family" questions I shared in the previous Chapter, and then... you're going to answer it in a "Reveal" format with your audience.

One of the Family questions in the last chapter was "Who loves you most in your family?" Let's say the answer was your grandma.

Now you're going to share something about "Grandma's love for you" in that "Reveal" format (think Jersey Shore Confessional Room). Maybe you share the moment you first realized how much your Grandma loved you, or you share one of your most cherished memories with her. Or maybe, you decide not to use "Reveal" as the Content Delivery Type and go with Public Journaling instead.

So you type out a public journal about how much your grandma loves you and how grateful you are for it and how you wish everyone could experience that kind of unconditional love in their life too.

For as long as you have a brand or online presence you can share genuine, unique connection-forming content with your audience everyday simply by choosing one category from the left side, and one from the top.

	Health	Travel	Business	Family	Entertainment	Food	Personal
Reveals							
Demo's							
Just Happeneds							
Live Look-In							
Public Journaling							
Rants							

Do you see how flexible this is? And how it makes the content easy? And how it ensures the Connection Content you're sharing fosters a bond and sense of closeness with your audience because it's all self-disclosing?

All these things that used to be such a challenge with social media for me, like…

- What Connection Content do I create?
- What's OK to share? What's not?
- I have no ideas today, what should I talk about or do?

- I'm not comfortable sharing this but I know it would really resonate. How do I do that?

…were no longer a challenge for me anymore after the Connection Twister. Creating and sharing Connection Content became easy and fun for me.

Like it's now going to be for you with the Connection Twister at your service.

11 COMMUNICATION

I was clueless about "monetizing social media" just a few years ago.

I had tens of thousands of followers at the time. Thousands of people liked my posts, and more people were messaging us each day. But we weren't really monetizing, at least not well. I thought I'd considered all the monetization options out there...

I didn't want to pimp out my audience for sponsorships (because then you're constantly sending your business to other companies and pretty soon, you're left with nothing). And we tried to monetize by doing "swipe ups" to a landing page but the click-thru rate wasn't great and our data showed "swipe-up traffic" was the lowest converting traffic we had.

Deep down, I knew there was so much more juice left to squeeze here but no clue how to do it. Have ever felt like that?

Around the same time, I'd hired Taki Moore (an amazing human who helps coaches increase their income and their time-off) to help me with the coaching part of my business.

I showed Taki that we had followers on social media but no good way to monetize.

He said, "Why don't you just do chat conversion?"

I asked, "What in the hell is chat conversion?"

Taki gets his phone, goes to his Facebook Messenger app and shows me what he meant by "Chat Conversion". It turned out, he and his team had been booking sales appointments all day long not by using funnels or emails or landing pages or webinars or VSL's but simply by *chatting with prospects.*

Just simple, basic chat. Having conversations with people. Like you do with your family or friends.

He said, "We get more than half our business via chat… remember Jason, conversions happen in conversations."

My eyes went wide as the moon.

The realization hit me all at once.

This was it.

This was how we were going to monetize on social media.

I immediately started testing all kinds of chat scripts and different ways to use the chat feature on Facebook Messenger and Instagram.

Nothing fancy.

Just having real, human conversations with people over the chat feature. But doing it in a way no one else on social media was doing.

We made an extra $8,000 the first month on our Instagram account and I was encouraged.

We made an extra $59,000 the second month on our Instagram account and I was pumped.

In the third month, we'd made an extra $102,000 on our Instagram account and I was officially no longer clueless.

It's gone up every month since, sales have never been better. And more customers means more impact.

As of today, we've deeply tested over 16 different ways to convert by chat and we've narrowed it down to a few winning methods. I'm going to share those with you in this chapter. We started calling these winning methods "Chat Engines" because of how much extra revenue they drive on social media.

I started teaching my audience Chat Conversion too, in a program called IG Agent. If you were to buy IG Agent, the idea is you'd learn Chat Conversion then offer to perform the service for local businesses, online stores and influencers/speakers/authors/coaches, etc, in exchange for commissions on sales made.

The very first student I taught this to was Eric Cipolla. On his first day, Eric made a $20,000 sale for his client using our Chat Engine. By the end of the first week, Eric had sold $60,000 for his client as an IG Agent. His commission was 20%. Eric had made $20,000 profit his very first week. The was more than Eric's parents made in a month. Like me, Eric dropped out of school and is making a healthy 6-figures today as an IG Agent.

There's one pretty big alligator we've seen when applying the Chat Engine to bigger social media accounts on Instagram that you should be aware of.

If you have an audience of more than 200,000 people on Instagram, you know that on a given day, hundreds of people may message you. When that happens everyday, managing and tracking all the chats on your own doesn't become "hard", it becomes impossible. (Especially when you throw in all the things required to really maximize the ROI of your audience, like you know, follow-up sequences, tagging prospects vs customers, segmentation, promotional calendars, not to mention the commissions you're paying your IG Agents and tracking all of that, especially if you have multiple IG Agents in your account, and if you're bigger than 200K, you will need multiple Agents to handle the volume.)

Basically, if you have a smaller audience (like under 100K), you'll probably be fine with one Agent and normal marketing tracking and reporting.

But if you're bigger than that and you don't want to leave 80% of your revenue on the table, you'll need to do a lot more to really let the Chat Engine drive this giant revenue stream for you (or, if it's a fit, talk to me about doing it for you).

I spoke at a marketing event last week in LA. Afterwards, I was showing another speaker what the chat activity looks like in my own Instagram. He couldn't believe the hundreds of active conversations all happening in that very moment. He said he had a friend with 4 Million followers and their chat looked nothing like ours, that ours was 20X more active.

I told him what I'll tell you: "What you see in our chat is the tip of the iceberg of what's making it work. To internally manage the chaos created by the sheer volume of having hundreds of conversations a day, we spent a ton of time and money to build software (which we weren't even sure would work, as is always the case with software). Plus we always need to make sure we're being compliant with the Instagram's Terms of Service which can be tricky. But on the good side, less than 1% of Influencers are even doing this. You'll be stoked at the revenue even a little bit of this Chat Engine stuff can drive on any type of account."

How much revenue can it drive?

In my Agency, we've begun to partner with big social media accounts who are a fit and apply our Chat Engine to their account for them.

My first "test subject" was a close friend. (He's asked we keep his name private since I'm sharing his actual data with you.) He had 250,000 followers on Instagram when we started. In the first 30 days, our Chat Engine team had driven an extra $121,000 in revenue, selling his products to his Instagram audience. My friend sent me the most amazing thank-you letter after because he didn't really have to do anything, this was "found money" for him that he's now getting everyday and frankly, my friend has an unbelievably important message, the more customers he gets, the better the world is. But what about your account and your offers?

If you had 1 Million followers on Instagram, in the first 30 days our Chat Engine team would have driven $448,000 in extra revenue for you. That's an extra $5.3 Million in the first year.

But what if you only have 100,000 followers on Instagram? In the first 30 days our Chat Engine team would have driven an extra $44,800 for you in the first 30 days. That's an extra $530,000 for you in Year 1.

What if you only had 10,000 followers? in the first 30 days our Chat Engine team would have driven an extra $4,800 for you in the first 30 days (or an extra $53,000 for you in Year 1).

All of this done at "no risk" to the client too. They don't have to put any time or money in. We just plug in to the client's account and handle everything. It's a great, great passive revenue stream for the client with a gigantic ceiling.

And if you're concerned that applying the Chat Engine to your account would take away from your other monetization strategies, there's no need to worry because it doesn't. The Chat Engine is a "bolt-on" revenue stream that starts driving new, extra sales the minute you begin.

Understand: We aren't "entering the Conversation Era", *we are in the Conversation Era*. It's here.

Last year, I took a vacation with Nataly to the Italian island of Capri. It is a magnificent paradise, and the people there are so friendly (and stylish).

Sitting down to eat at a local cafe, I noticed a photograph hanging up of Jay-Z and Beyonce eating at the same restaurant (apparently the owner had snapped the photo and Jay didn't like it because he looked miserable in the photo). I asked our waiter about it and he said, "Yes, that Mr. Jay-Z did not want his picture taken! But we got it anyways!"

Then he pointed to the photo next to it. It was a photo of a statue of a man I didn't recognize. He asked, "Do you know who that is though?"

"I have no clue who that is."

He replied, "That is the Roman Emperor Tiberius. He ruled the empire from Capri, and legend has it he built "sex castles" all over the island for his own pleasure."

Intrigued (naturally), I googled Tiberius and, "sex castles" aside, I learned that while living on the tiny island of Capri, the Roman Emperor Tiberius had ruled all of Rome by inventing the first telecommunications in the history of mankind. How?

Tiberius did it by signaling messages to Rome with metal mirrors that reflected the sun.

That was 2,000 years ago.

After Tiberius, telecommunications evolved. First came the telegraph… then Morse Code… then the first telephone… then the first radio and TV… then computers and mobile phones. Along the way, entrepreneurs found ways to use these inventions to broadcast their marketing message to the world. And it worked.

But for the first time in 2,000 years, marketing has changed forever.

Until now, you made an ad and put it in the newspaper, or on the radio, or on TV, or on Google or Facebook, and you let that ad yell from the rooftops how great your product or service was.

Today, the best way to convert prospects into customers, and get your message out there isn't to have your marketing yell at them but to *have actual conversations with your audience.*

Not bots, not automation but real humans having real conversations with other real humans via chat.

Because conversions happen in conversations.

Why not just have phone calls with your prospects? Aren't billions of dollars sold over the phone every year?

They sure are. And I expect that to continue. But not forever..

My friend Kevin Hutto has booked over 80,000 sales calls in the last few years. His data shows "show rates for phone appointments are now lower than ever".

I hold seminars, sometimes with over 1,000 people in attendance, and I always ask, "How many of you would prefer a brand or business to chat with you instead of call you?" More than 95% of hands go up for "chat" every time.

Look at ourselves. Someone calls us, and we go, "Why are you calling me? Just send me a text."

We prefer chat because it's on our time. We get to decide when we reply. With a phone appointment, you don't have that same freedom.

And when you compare chat to email, it's a joke. A good email open rate is 20%. Chat gets open rates of 90%-95%.

I could go on and on here but I feel like the stage has been set, and I want to show you how the Chat Engine is going to drive all kinds of extra revenue for you and your business in this Section.

Welcome to the Conversation Era.

Let's go.

12 SOCIAL MEDIA CALL-TO-ACTION'S

I'd just sent Hilary Clinton $1,000.

I couldn't believe I'd done it.

But I did.

It was 2015, and I was on the Hilary Clinton For President website. I'd just donated $1,000 to her campaign. Why so shocked at what I'd done?

1. I'm not into politics at all. Why the hell would I be donating money to a candidate?

2. If I was into politics, I would not be giving my money to Hilary Clinton.

So why do it?

Earlier that day, I'd taught a private personal development workshop to about 50 customers. The workshop was an introductory workshop, meaning I'd teach the audience all the foundations of strong personal development, then deliver a strong call-to-action to ascend them into a more advanced, more personal, more expensive workshop at the end.

Except I didn't do that.

When the end of the workshop came and it was time for my big upsell call-to-action, I wussed out. I told myself I'd developed such a good connection with this audience that.. to sell them.. would demean the connection. It'd be disrespectful. It'd be greddy. Blah blah blah. I couldn't have been more wrong, here's why:

The more advanced workshop I was supposed to sell them was better than the introductory workshop. They would have gotten more out of it (because they would have been prepared to handle the more advanced stuff). For those willing to take action, that advanced workshop could have been their bridge to truly living a kick-ass life. I stole that chance from them, by not offering them the chance to sign-up for it.

On the drive home, I was kicking myself for bitching out. So I made a deal with myself: I would never "wuss out" on making a strong call-to-action ever again. And to put my money where my mouth was (and to punish myself), I donated $1,000 to Hilary Clinton, someone I absolutely did not want running the USA as President. And now 4 years later, I'm proud to say that:

1. 1) I have never *not* made a strong call-to-action since. I've stood by my word.

2. 2) My $1,000 wasn't enough to get Hilary elected.

Humor me for a second: Can we both agree that the product or service you sell is GREAT? And would be a huge value-add to the customer? Yes? And can we also both agree that tomorrow's not promised? I know, tomorrow's *probably* going to happen, and it's *highly-probable* the sun will rise tomorrow but.. it's not going to rise for all of us - 151,000 human beings will take their final breath sometime today.

Here's my point: Since your product/service is great.. and since tomorrow's truly not promised for all of your audience or mine, don't we have a duty to do everything we can to get our solution in the customer's hands today?

Imagine if it wasn't just a Call-To-Action but our audience's final chance for a better quality of life? And our *final chance* to help them get there? What kind of heat would you bring to your Call-To-Action's then?

I'm hammering this point home because I see so many influencer's dropping the ball on their call-to-action... and costing themselves sales everytime.

The Call-To-Action acts as the bridge our audience crosses from prospect to paying customer, and the core problems I currently see are:

- weak call-to-action (selling from your heels instead of your toes, too much "aww shucks")
- formulaic call-to-action (no heart, no soul, no sense that you care)
- no trust embedded inside the call-to-action
- no social proof leveraged during the call-to-action
- no urgency (in their tone or their words)
- no call-to-action at all (just hoping that people figure out which link to click)

Listen, I've been a dedicated student of online marketing for 12 years now. I was fortunate to be making money from Day One but I've never stopped being a lifetime student. I am always working on improving my call-to-action's. You should be too.

I like to joke the first call-to-action ever was Moses leading his people out of Egypt. The Pharaoh is hot on their tale. They get to the Red Sea, nowhere to go. They're like...fvck. Then Moses gives a great Dramatic Demonstration (parting the Red Sea) and makes a great call-to-action for everyone to follow him across. And so they do, barely evading Pharaoh's grasp, en route to safe land.

Call-to-actions matter. A lot.

Friends simply don't let friends get away with crappy CTA's.

Here are the key principles to Call-To-Action's that actually get your followers to take action:

Don't Be a Starfish

Here's the story: Buddy I know goes to Vegas. Meets a dancer (he's single). She's whispering sweet-nothings in his ear. They go to his hotel room. Things heat up. And then he, as he says, proceeds to "have the most boring love-making of his life". (He didn't say it quite so PG-13.) But he did say it was like "making love with a starfish...she just laid there".

I tell this story because we don't want you to be that Starfish either (with your marketing and sales!). You're doing all this work to warm up your audience. But we both know nothing happens until that person in your audience takes action. Let's not be the Starfish who's all talk but loses steam at the end with a call-to-action that doesn't deliver.

Keep the Benny's

Depending on what type of Call-To-Action you're making, the data shows it's usually best to infuse a benefit into the Call-To-Action. This would be you saying, "Click the link below *to start burning extra fat today*" instead of just saying "Click the link below to get started now". Imagine I'm the prospect here. The first Call-To-Action makes me want to click it, the second doesn't pack the same persuasion punch.

Clarity is Power

Confused mind's don't buy. I see so many brands and influencers who confuse the crap out of their prospect. "Click the link. Tag 3 people. Comment on 4 posts. And do this all in the next 10 seconds." It's not that the prospect isn't willing to do all that for you but confusion equals pain, and people move away from pain. You want your Call-To-Action's to be *anti-confusion*. I don't care if this is a caption, copy or a video. Remember that term: Anti-confusion.

Remaining Their #1 Advocate

With the Credibility and Connection content you're sharing, your audience is starting to see you as their #1 Advocate - their hero. But when it comes time to sell, a lot of Influencer's will perform this miraculous "Dr. Jekyll/ Mr. Hyde maneuver" and suddenly turn into a Billy Mays infomercial. You know, yapping on and on about the features, benefits, overcoming objections and let's not forget the huge discount we have in store for you today. Yikes. You go from "advocate mode" to "used car salesperson mode", and your audience is left wondering, "Wait...do I trust this person or not?"

Here's my rule: I connect my Call-To-Action to the Vision. For instance, with my audience right now, the big vision is helping them replace rat-race life with laptop life. So I don't ramble on about the discounts, bonuses and benefits, I just connect the Call-To-Action with the main vision, and that's it. It might sound like, "Swipe up to join the hundreds of others who have already begun to replace rat-race life with laptop life by watching this new video". That's it. The goal of this Call-To-Action isn't to close the sale, it's to get them to take the next action, whether that be clicking a link, swiping up, or messaging me.

Something Bigger

People are bored. Boring breakfast. Boring work. Boring workout. Boring dinner. Boring TV shows. It's a lot of bored people searching for something not boring. We need to ensure our Call-To-Action's, our sales, our promotions are not boring either. My best tactic for this is to make the promotion part of something bigger than just "buying this shirt" or "ordering this supplement". For example, you can turn the "order my supplement" Call-To-Action into "I'm accepting 100 people into this Pilot Program, where you'll take the supplement everyday and we'll track your results for the next 30 days together". Do you see how much more interesting that appeal is? Other good ways to do this include using ideas like a Guinea Pig Program, Beta Tester's, Test Group, Case Study, Scholarships, Financial Aid Program, Special Experiment, 30-Day Challenge, Internship Application or Become A Brand Ambassador.

Now that you've got the formula to Call-To-Action's that actually get your audience to act, it's time for the next part of Communication -- the Chat Engine.

13 CHAT ENGINES

We're in the Conversation Era.

You know you need to be having real (not automated) conversations with your followers.

You know conversions happen in conversations.

And you know the more conversations you have, the more conversions you can have. Which means more sales, more customers and more impact. This is all part of the system we call the Chat Engine.

But what should you be saying to your fans and followers? How long should the conversations be? What questions should you ask? What questions should you *never* ask? What things should you *never* say? How do you know when they're ready for a CTA? Or to make a purchase? Does the Chat Engine work like phone sales but just a chat conversation instead of a phone conversation? I'm going to answer all these questions for you in this chapter, and more.

Before I do, let me cover a few sticking points I've heard from other Influencers about turning their followers into one of the greatest revenue streams ever.

"But Jason, I don't want to appear salesy to my audience?"

Neither do I.

We've both seen some big accounts that sell everyday and seem to do OK with it. That's fine but since they haven't put the Chat Engine to work in their business, they're probably driving only 25% of the revenue they could be right now.

Then there's accounts I see that do their best to balance the content-to-pitch ratio. It's usually something like 80% content, 20% pitch. Some people call it the 80/20 Content Rule. That can work fine too but if you're only pitching 20% of the time, you're only monetizing 20% of the time.

I used to follow something like the 80/20 Content Rule too, and I knew it wasn't ideal. Sales would spike only a couple days of the week and the other days would be slow. If you do the 80/20 thing and you're reading this, you know you're missing out on a whole bunch of revenue on those days you only share content with no selling. But you still believe, "I can't sell my audience everyday, they'd get annoyed, see me only as a salesman and get turned off." Which is *probably* true.

That's what's so magical about installing the Chat Engine into your social media business. With the Chat Engine, you're never *publicly* selling to your audience. You're never telling them "the deadline is tonight or "the product's 25% Off for the rest of the day" or hard-selling at all.

Imagine that..

Imagine never publicly selling to your audience ever again..

Imagine all the love and adoration if you just gave, gave, gave to them…

And now imagine making 2X, 3X or 5X as much revenue as you are right now, as a result of only giving in public…

With the Chat Engine, that's what we do. Taki Moore taught me to only "give in public, ask in private" and that's what we're doing here.

Because all the conversions don't happen from the copy in your caption or videos, or from you telling them to "swipe up". All the conversions happen in conversations, in the messaging part of the app, in private. And because it's in private in the chat, the rest of your audience never sees the selling part.

"But Jason, I don't want to really sell my audience and besides, I don't have anything good to sell to my audience."

Can I be blunt? This attitude worries me. It's too short-sighted.

I've been marketing online for 12 years. I've seen a lot of people build online empires only to fade away after a couple years, or have to go back to a 9-5. Wanna know the difference? The ones who have empires believe selling is one of the most noble things you can do for another human, and so they sell all the time.

Let's say you have an audience right now and you don't want to annoy them or come off "salesy" so you rarely sell, and when you do, it's a pitch so soft you could slice it with a butter knife. You think you're being a "good person" but really you're being selfish as hell. You're more concerned with what your audience thinks of you than serving them.

Think about your audience: Do you think every problem in their life is solved? That their life is picture-perfect, a never-ending stream of love, joy, happiness, satisfaction and unicorns? Of course not. They still have challenges and frustrations and if you really cared about them, you'd be doing everything in your power to solve those problems for them WITH YOUR PRODUCTS OR SERVICES.

Sorry, I didn't mean to go "all caps" on you but I just feel so passionate about this.

Refusing to sell is selfish. What refusing to sell really says is you care more about what the other person thinks of you than you care about helping that other person improve their life. That's selfish. And you are not a selfish person.

I believe we all have gifts and talents and those gifts and talents do not belong to us, they belong to the community. It's our path to cultivate those gifts and talents and share them with the world. But people value a thing by the price they paid to acquire that thing. If you just give your products or services away for free, people won't value them and therefore, won't use them.

This is why we sell. This is why entrepreneurs, marketers and sales people matter. A lot. Without us, business doesn't happen and neither does customer transformation. If the world was a bike, we're the ones moving the pedals forward. We have *the* most important role.

And what if you have nothing to sell your audience? Here's what I don't do: I don't assume I know what my audience wants and try to sell that to them. Isn't it disrespectful to assume you know what someone else wants? And yet 95% of marketers still do this. Instead, I ask my audience questions like:

- What would you like my help with right now?
- If you could change one thing about your business, what would it be? (you could replace business with health, relationships, marketing, etc)
- What's the most frustrating part about your business right now?
- What's something you know you should do but keep putting off? (If I can do the thing they've been putting off *for them*, I've got an instant customer)

My friend Justin Goff advises some of the biggest players in the online health space. He gave me a great tip for figuring out what to offer your audience. He said, "Make a list of 7 offers you think your audience would want to buy. Then survey them. List out the 7 offers for them and ask them for each offer, "Would you buy this?" The offer people say they'd buy the most is the one you offer."

"But Jason, my audience is different, they won't buy over chat, I don't see this working for me."

Can I share a secret? Even though in my previous life, my title said "America's Honest Dating Coach", I wasn't really a dating coach. I was in personal development. I helped guys develop into the most powerful, most resourceful, highest-status version of themselves. And in that time, I saw everything. It was not just teaching guys how to pick up chicks.

I helped a 72-year old and recently widowed Harvard PhD, who thought his life was over, attract the love of his life and marry her. He told me now at 72, life was just beginning for him.

I helped hundreds of guys lose 50 or 100 lbs just by installing simple success principles no one had ever taught them.

I'm proud to say, I even talked several guys who were suicidal off the ledge and turn their entire lives around.

My point is this: People everywhere want the same things. Dr. Joe Vitalte says there are 10 universal human motivators, and they are:

- Security
- Happiness
- Sex
- Safety
- Power
- Health
- Immortality
- Recognition
- Wealth
- Love

Your audience is not different.

We may sell different products but our customers are buying these products because *some video, some message, some conversation* has caused them to believe our product is the vehicle that will drive them to one (or more) of those 10 human motivators.

Now let's get into how to apply the Chat Engine to your social media.

There's 3 parts to the Chat Engine:

1. Prompt
2. Chat
3. Convert

First, we're going to *Prompt* our audience to message us so we can have that conversation with them. Remember, conversions happen in conversations.

Next, we're going to *Chat* with them. But we're not just going to have any chat with them. We're going to follow a framework that I've found to work remarkably well in getting them to buy.

Finally, we're going to *Convert* them from a follower or prospect into a customer. The first time you get a new customer doing this, you're going to be amazed, and maybe stunned. Then pretty soon, you're going to wonder how you ever did business before without the Chat Engine.

Prompt

This is the easiest part of the Chat Engine. All you do here is simply tell your audience to message you. People are always so stunned when I tell them this. "You mean it's that easy Jason? I just tell them to message me?" My answer is yes.

But why *should* they message you? You need to give them an incentive. Here are some examples you can put to use:

- "We just added a new necklace to the collection and we're looking for a few people to be first to wear them and let us know what they think. If you're interested, just send me a message and I'll send you the details."
- "We have 12 extra tinctures of our best CBD in stock and I want to get rid of them today at a big time discount. Send me a message when you see this and if you're one of the first 12 to message me, I'm gonna hook you up big time."
- "I just made a great new hire in my business and they've opened up my schedule so I now have room to take on 1 more client who wants me to work closely with them. If that's you, just message me so we can chat."

As you can see, it's not rocket science. All of these messages have a few things in common:

1. There's a story. It's in Hollywood what they would call an "inciting incident". Something's just happened that caused this opportunity to open up.
2. There's a "reason why" you're doing it. You want people to test the necklaces. You want to get rid of extra CBD. You just hired someone new and it freed up your time.
3. There's limited availability. You're only looking for a few people to try the necklaces. You only have 12 tinctures of CBD in stock. You have room for 1 new client.

4. It's easy for the prospect to take the next step. This isn't Indiana Jones and you're not asking them to identify the one cup out of 20 that doesn't have poison in it. All they have to do is message you. Just type a few buttons and hit send. They never even have to leave whatever platform you're doing this on too since messaging features are native to their platform. (This might be the most important part, by the way. Friction kills conversions. I'm always looking for way to make our conversion process more friction-free.)

5. This wasn't included in the examples, but we've had a lot of success telling our audience a specific word to message us. For example, "message me the word "tiger" and I'll get you all the details". The word you choose does not matter. It works because if you tell them to message you but don't give them a word to message you with, some people will go to message you then realize they don't know exactly what to say. And instead of possibly looking silly by sending you the wrong message, they won't message you altogether. Silly, I know. But true. So if you give them a specific thing to do or say when they reach out to you, you should get even more people to respond. Your mileage may vary.

Chat

Now you have people messaging you, interested in what you got going on...but what do you say back to them? Welcome to the wonderful world of The 6 Boxes.

I have tested out over 16 different "chat scripts" and different ways to warm prospects up over chat. And over time, I found The 6 Boxes just crushed it internally for us but it's not just us. Remember my friend, who was the first influencer I partnered up with to build a whole Chat Engine for? We made an extra $121,000 in the first 30 days for him using The 6 Boxes I'm about to share with you too. In fact, some of my students love The 6 Boxes so much they had t-shirts printed that said "6-Box God" on them.

The 6 Boxes looks like this:

After the person messages you, you're going to start with the first Box "Situation". This is where you let the prospect set the stage for where they're at in their business, life, health, relationships, etc. You simply say, "So tell me a little about your situation right now". You'll be amazed at how much that little statement brings out of the prospect. Some will write you a novel. (Sidenote: When a prospect writes you a "novel", that's a good thing. It means they're keen to get help.)

After they tell you their Situation, you go to the next Box "Gap". This is where we let the prospect tell us where they're at and where they'd like to be (hence the name, the "Gap"). Most prospects won't buy a solution unless they recognize there's a problem. And if there's a gap between where they want to be and where they're currently at, that's a problem. That's why this Box is so important. And all you say is something like, "I'm curious, where would you like your business to be 90 days from now? And where's it at now?" Depending on your industry and what you sell, you probably won't say "where would you like your business to be". If you sell fat loss, you might say, "Where would you like your weight to be 90 days from now?". If you sell clothes, you might want to use a different Gap question. I have a student who sells high-end fashion wear and has had a lot of success asking, "Why do you want this sweatshirt over the ones you have now?" The point is your question in the Gap Box compels the prospect to realize there's a Gap.

The third Box is "Missing". This is where we let the prospect tell us what's missing. In sales copy, this is similar to the "Agitate" part of the famous Problem-Agitate-Solution copywriting framework. We do this by asking, "So what do you think is missing right now?" It's incredible how people will just tell you what they believe is missing. And the more emotional intensity they have about what they feel is missing, the more likely they'll be to buy with less price resistance too. And please save this persuasion insight somewhere safe: People resist what they're told but never doubt what they conclude. When you ask them "What's missing?" and they answer, you're not the one telling them what's missing. If you did, they might have doubts. But since we're letting them tell us what's missing, the diagnosis is of their volition, they're the one who said, not us, and so their belief level is that much higher as a result.

The fourth Box is "Need". This is where we let the prospect tell us what they think they need. This is key because whatever they tell you they need, you're going to tie that back in when it comes time for the conversion. For example, if I'm selling something "work from home" and they tell me they "need accountability because they've tried working from home in the past and they end up watching soap operas all day", then when I go to convert, I can add in a sentence about all the personal accountability they'll get so even if they want to watch Days of Our Lives instead of make money from home, we won't let them. Does that make sense? And for this Box, all you say is, "So what do you feel you need most from me right now?"

The fifth Box is Priority. Have you ever had someone tell you "I'm gonna buy today" and then they don't for 3 weeks? Or they never buy? What if that almost never happened with a lead again? That's what the 5th Box "Priority" does. Here, we pin the prospect down to a timeline. We say, "Now before we talk next step, I just need to check-in, would you say getting this situation handled is a priority for you, or something you'll just get to later?" If they answered your first few questions, it's been clearly established they have a problem that needs solving. They know it and you know it. So it'd be embarrassing for them, after all that, to tell you "Yeah, I know it's important and a problem but I'm just gonna ignore it for a while and get to it later". Nearly everyone says, "Yes, this is a priority for me" in response to this Box and now the urgency part is handled.

The sixth and final Box is the "Lifejacket". After the answers they gave you in the first 5 boxes, you can imagine the prospect is kind of feeling lost at sea right about now. We also know if we want to, and can, help them, or not. If we do, then here we offer them a lifejacket. This is the transition to Conversion. And it's so simple. Nothing salesy at all. You say, "Would you like some help with that?" And it's beautiful, because almost everyone says "Yes" to that question, and now they've given us permission to convert them from prospect to customer.

A quick side note before we get to the final section here. You may not need all 6 Boxes in every conversation you have. Sometimes, we'll ask the first Box "Situation" and the prospect will naturally answer the Gap, Missing and Need Box all in one answer. Other times, you offer a product that doesn't need all 6 Boxes to convert. In those cases, you can just shrink it down to "The 3 Boxes". With some of our clients in those cases, we'll just use "Situation-Gap-Help" as the 3 Box framework.

Convert

Convert is the fun part. This is where we generate revenue and start making a real impact on the customer's life via our product or service. And there's a few ways you can make the final conversion, after they tell you they want your help:

- You can simply sell them the product or service via Chat. I follow a simple framework that works great for this. I just tell them what the offer is, what promise it'll provide them, I back up that promise with proof (via testimonials, case studies, success stories etc) and then I make a Friction-Free Offer for them to get started easily, including a reason why they need to get started today, and not later. Remember, today's marketplace is the Convenience Marketplace. You're going to lose sales if buying your product or service is at all inconvenient to the prospect. Pro Tip: Instead of typing this simple "Promise/Proof/Friction-Free Offer", try recording it as a personal video inside of the platform and send it to the prospect that way. Some prospects, especially younger ones, are more used to watching than reading so video can often convert even better than written word. And this is chat. Keep the messages short. Even when I do a full "Promise/Proof/Friction-Free Offer", it'll only be a few sentences max. If it's a video, it'll usually be under a minute. If they have more questions, let them ask you instead of trying to jam all the information into the offer.

- You can send them to a landing page or order form where they can purchase the offer. Use the "Promise/Proof/Friction-Free Offer" formula on the landing page too. Remind them why they're buying. This could be short copy, or a video above the order form. Another Pro Tip: If you audience is small enough and you have the time to do it (or if you're selling something high-ticket enough that it justifies the extra time cost), create a unique landing page for *each* individual prospect, with *THEIR NAME* in big bold letters at the top. A little personalization will do wonders for your conversions.

- You can send them to a private landing page with a surprise discount. My more aggressive marketers will like this one. In this case, it's just like the example above but you also include a surprise discount. For example, if in the Chat, you told them it's $497 and then they land on the page and there's a headline that says, "Surprise Discount Today Only: Save An Extra $100 Off By Placing Your Order Today!" It'll work even better if you add a countdown timer to the page too.

You're really unlimited in your options here. Be creative. My team and I have an entire R & D department for this. We are always testing new ways to convert prospects in the chat and whenever we find a new winning formula, we apply it to all of your client's accounts and the results are consistently epic.

"In winning, there are no big things. There are only a lot of little things done well which add up to big things." - John Wooden

I want to give you a few more key elements to the Chat Engine. The first is how you send the messages.

Look at the difference between these two messages, what do you notice?

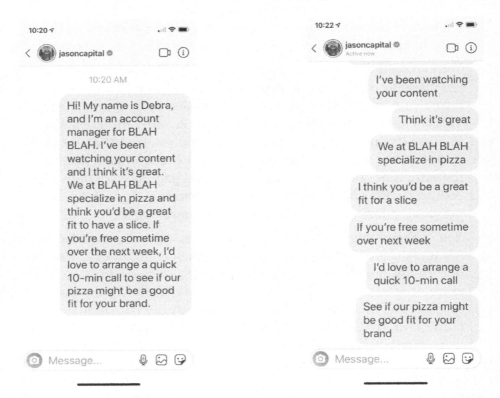

The messages have the same words but they say different things.

The first is one large block of text. It looks like the sender spent a ton of time working on it. It smells like neediness. And causes your recipient's "guard" to go up. The large block of text is also intimidating to the recipient. ("There's no way I'm going to read all this.")

The second is cut up into a bunch of shorter messages. It doesn't look premeditated. Instead, it looks spontaneous. And casual. (Both of which make it so the recipient's guard does not go up.) It's also not intimidating. It's a quick, breezy read for even the most distractible of folk.

We call this "texting like a 14-year old girl". If you have a teenage daughter, have her show you how her and her friends message each other. It's not long blocks of text. It's quick barrage of messages, one after another. This is how you want your chats to be.

Yes.

I'm serious.

You want your chats to look like those of a 14-year old girl.

We've tested this out a lot.

Test it for yourself if you don't believe me.

Another key detail:

I know I didn't paint "phone sales" in the best light before but if you're doing big transactions, like 6-figure or 7-figure deals, you should nudge them on the phone to convert but when you do, you'll notice the prospect is infinitely warmer *because of the relationship that was built in the chat first.*

The last note I want to make here is what you say *in between each of the 6 Boxes*. If you're just going from asking one question to the next, it'll feel too formal to the prospect, too much like an interview and that'll kill the rapport.

We use a simple formula between each Box called "EP" which stands for Empathy and Proof. All it means is after each answer get from the prospect, we EP it for a second before moving on to the next Box.

Visually, it looks like this:

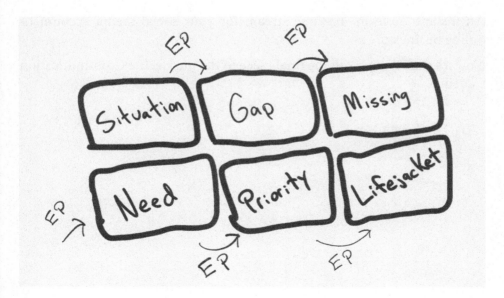

For example, let's say I asked you the first Box Question ("Situation"), and you told me, "My social media is doing pretty well. We make about a $1 per follower, not near the $5-$10 per follower you guys do, but we do all right. I feel there's more we could do but I'm not sure what."

If I just ignored your answer and went straight to asking you the 2nd Box Question, it'd be weird. You'd feel unheard and there's no faster way to make someone feel like they don't matter than ignoring what they just said.

So instead, I'd use a little EP *then* I'd move on to the 2nd Box.

I could say, "I totally hear you on that (Empathy Statement). When I was first starting out, we were doing about $1 per follower too but I felt like I was always selling, I didn't like it. It feels better now to do $5 per follower and never have to sell (Proof). So you told me you're at $1 per follow now, where do you think that number could be 90 days from now?" See what we're doing here? I reply first with a quick Empathy statement, then some Proof, then I go right into the 2nd Box Question.

So now you have The Chat Engine.

The Engine that's driven millions and millions of dollars for Influencers in only a few months without interfering or taking away from any of their other promotional or monetization strategies.

An instant "bolt-on" revenue stream for your social media account or online business.

Now it's time to give you the final piece to the puzzle, the Communication Cadence.

A PUBLIC SERVICE ANNOUNCEMENT ABOUT SITTING ON A GOLDMINE AND LEAVING MONEY ON THE TABLE.

Please remember, if you're 100K followers or less, I believe you can crush the Chat Engine on your own. The chat volume may be high at times but if you've got the time to dedicate to it, you can crush it. If you're over 100K followers or more and you have engaged audience, you can drive great revenue too but due to sheer volume of messages you'll be receiving and people you'll be chatting with, you will lose track of 50-80% of your prospects and lose 50-80% of revenue as a result. With the number of big Influencer accounts I've been behind the scenes of, I'd have to be an idiot not to see this pattern of massive amounts of revenue being left on the table. If you're an influencer with more than 100K engaged followers, you are sitting on a goldmine right now and frankly, I don't know how long it will last. Could be 1 year, could be 10 years. Not to pitch my services here, because I'm a bit curmudgeonly and picky about my clients (I feel like I have to be since we spend so much time together), but if you have an account that's bigger than 100K followers and the followers are engaged.. and you can handle an extra $25,000 - $100,000 a month in revenue without you having to lift a finger, you will probably make a lot more money and help a lot more people by just letting my team do all this for you. End rant.

14 CONTENT

How do we get a great result?

We follow a great process.

Like my friend Sharran Srivatsaa says, "Good process drives good results." Sharran should know. He used a specific set of processes to grow his real estate company by 10X to $3.4 Billion. (And he 10X'ed it in only 5 years.)

Ever been to South Pole? Me neither.

Roald Amundsen was the first man to reach the South Pole in 1911.

Another explore, Robert Scott, tried to beat Amundsen to it.

Both Amundsen and Scott began their voyage around the same time, and faced similar weather conditions. But Scott got there a month earlier, and made it home safely. Amundset froze to death on the way back, and his body was found 10 miles from the nearest storage depot. What was the difference?

Amundsen was infinitely more *prepared* than Scott.

Amundsen apprenticed under Eskimo's before his journey. He learned to walk slowly in the cold (otherwise you sweat, and the sweat freezes). He also brought so many supplies for him and his men, they could have gone 100 extra miles and been fine. Scott did not prepare like this. In fact, if Scott's team missed just one supply depot, it would have spelled disaster for him and his team. (And it did.)

I'm not going to waste your time with "failing to plan is planning to fail" quotes in regards to making your social media really pop. You know this.

But knowing is not enough. We must apply what we know. And even applying is not enough. We must inject what we know directly into the large vein of social media to ensure the things we want to happen, happen.

I have two French bulldogs, Kennedy and Sterling.

If Kennedy and Sterling were running their own social media account, they wouldn't have a plan of what to post and when. There'd be no strategy. They'd just post whenever cool shit happened. I'd feed them dinner and before eating, they'd say, "Hold on one second Jason, I'm gonna post this meal to Instagram because it looks exquisite." Their posting would be random and inconsistent.

You are not a dog. You have the ability to plan, to strategize, to set an intention and follow through. So that's what we're going to do here.

This means no more missed posts. No more inconsistency. No more randomness with our posts.

In this Chapter, we're going to bake *everything* we've learned here together..

- Your Credibility Content
- Your Connection Content
- Your Call-To-Action's
- The Chat Engine

…into one recipe you can follow without a hitch, by following the Content Calendar. Here's what it's going to look like:

Monday

You're going to share Connection Content. That content is going to include a CTA for more engagement (comment, like, share, etc).

Tuesday

You're going to share Credibility Content. That content is going to include a CTA for your audience to message you, so you can apply the Chat Engine and let it drive all kinds of new revenue for you. You're also going to use Story's (IG, FB, etc) to Prompt more members of your audience to message you and really fill that Chat Pipeline.

Wednesday

You're going to share Connection Content. Include a CTA for more engagement as well. Do your best to respond and connect with everyone who engages too.

Thursday

Credibility Content. Include a CTA for your audience to message you. And use Story's to Prompt more of your audience to message you so the Chat Engine can do it's work for your revenue and sales.

Friday

Connection Content. Include a CTA for more engagement as well. I know it's Friday but still, do your best to respond and connect with everyone who engages with you. These are real people who by this point, are really starting to feel close to you as an Influencer and they deserve your recognition. I believe giving this type of personal attention and recognition to your engaged followers is a wise business move too *because assholes don't win in the social media economy.*

Saturday

Credibility Content. Include a CTA for your audience to message you as well.

Sunday

Connection Content. Include a CTA for more engagement as well. And post another Story to Prompt more people to message you so we keep fueling that Chat Engine with more and more prospects.

And that's it. Simple enough that you'll stick to it but as you know, there's a lot of strategy and psychology going on underneath the surface.

Some key points about the Content Calendar:

It Alternates Each Week

In the example I gave above, you'd be sharing 4 pieces of Connection Content and 3 pieces of Credibility Content each week. If that's the case, the following week you'd share 4 pieces of Credibility Content and 3 pieces of Connection Content.

You're Using The 6-Boxes (or 3 Boxes) All the While

While all this is going on, lots and lots of people are going to be messaging you, interested in your offer or new opportunity. Great! You should be chatting with them behind-the-scenes, using the 6 Boxes, or the 3 Boxes if it's a better fit, and converting them from prospect to customer.

You Can Do More If You Want

In this Content Calendar example, you're only posting once a day to your main social media accounts (which is Instagram or Facebook for most). You can post more if you want or have the resources to do so. My team and I post 3 times a day right now on Instagram.

But how much is too much? Can you post too much?

When I was 20 and just starting my online marketing career, I got invited to a private mastermind for marketers. There were about 40 people in the room, all of them much more experienced and successful than me. But they were all complaining about email open rates.

"My email open rates are going down…"

"No one opens my emails anymore…"

"Email marketing just isn't what it used to be…"

(What's funny is today, in 2020, people are still registering the same complaints about email marketing they were in 2009. In case you were wondering, yes, email marketing has changed, but no, it's not dead. It works great, for those who know what they're doing. My buddy Joel Marion generates over $80 Million a year via email marketing.)

Anyway.

There I was, this young kid, listening to a bunch of millionaire marketers whine and moan about email marketing. Finally, when they were done, one guy, who had been quiet until then, spoke up. His name was Ryan, and he was the biggest baller in the room.

He calmly shared, "Your email lists aren't dead. People are still reading email. But if they're not opening or reading, it's because you're not talking about their problems or frustrations or the things that interest them. Go back to talking about what they care about and they'll start reading again."

I never forgot that advice. It applies to social media too.

As long as you're creating or sharing content that your audience actually CARES about, you really can't post too much.

15 YOUR MESSAGE MATTERS

We're almost near the end and I'd love to share a message with you that on the surface seems like it has nothing to do with social media.

I recently got an email from someone who followed me.

They wanted their name kept private but part of their email said this..

"Four months ago, I was planning a trip to the mountains to end my life. Today, the sun is shining. I started a new business and it's thriving. There's a new woman in my life and we are smitten with each other. Speaking of women, I had gone 8 years without talking to my mom because I held onto so much anger at her from when I was younger but now we're talking multiple times a week and we even have a weekly lunch date. Your videos and trainings impacted me on a deep level, Jason. I would love to come to one of your live events and just shake your hand."

I believe, as Influencers, we're not just "posting content" or "building a brand".

We're breathing life into the world.

How do you feel as you read this?

151,000 people will die today.

That's a true statistic.

I know, it's a little dark to think about how many people will take their final breath today and yet there's a good chance it won't be you.

You still have time.

A lot of time.

Time to take action… implement… take your brand and business to the top of your industry… and leave this place better than you found it.

It doesn't matter if you've tried other stuff and felt it didn't work.

Learned helplessness is for dogs. You are not a dog.

I've "failed" at tons of things. My secret is not calling it a failure but an insight.

I "failed" at playing professional basketball. (I never made it.)

I "failed" at two businesses this year.

I've failed at at least 7 businesses in my career (so far).

I once hired a barista from Starbucks to run my entire company, because I was too overwhelmed and just needed help.

What I realize looking back now is none of those instances were failures. They were building blocks of experience - clay I could use to sculpt what's next. So are your experiences.

That's the marvelous thing about being human: we're in control. We can change our approach. Birds fly south in the winter. They can't help it. We can.

We can live one way for 5 years and then tear up that script one day and immediately start doing things differently, if we want. We get to write our own story.

Let's not be the author who forgot *they're the one holding the pen.*

As you go off and implement, I want to tell you about a hero of mine, Coach John Wooden, and his rule, which we call "Wooden's Rule".

John Wooden was the head basketball coach at UCLA for 27 seasons.

In those 27 seasons, his team won the national championship 10 times, including one period where they won the championship 7 years in a row.

(No team has ever won more than 4 in a row.)

If you've never played basketball, it works like almost every other sport: You win by scoring more points than your opponent, before the clock strikes zero.

Now get this: John Wooden, the coach with the most championships, never cared about the score. He taught his players not to care about the score either.

How is it *the guy who won the most* didn't care about winning?

Because John Wooden had different criteria for success than 99% of the population.

When another coach would face John Wooden, the other coach's goal was to out-score John Wooden.

But when John Wooden would face that other coach, Wooden's goal was for his team to give each moment their best effort. Wooden didn't care about the scoreboard, and didn't talk about the scoreboard. And yet *his teams won more than any other in history.*

Wooden said, "My dad taught me never try to be better than someone else. And never cease trying to be the best you can be - that's under your control. I ran across this simple verse that said, "At God's footstool to confess, a poor soul knelt, and bowed his head. "I failed!" he cried. The Master said, "Thou didst thy best, that is success."

How easy is it to get caught in the game of comparison on social media?

My advice is to follow Wooden's Rule:

Don't invest in trying to be better than someone else.

And never cease trying to be the best you can be.

Compete with your potential, not their clout.

As the billionaire Warren Buffet advises, "We do our best when we keep our eye on the field, not the scoreboard."

It's wonderful advice for being happy and tapping into the true heights of your potential but it's also superb advice for how to become *the* leader in your industry, for decades to come. (I hope the success of people like John Wooden and Warren Buffet will allow you to see that too.)

16 WHERE DO WE GO FROM HERE?

Phew!

At this moment you're probably feeling a little bit overwhelmed. This book was not meant to be casual reading for the casual reader. You've just completed a deep-dive immersion into some very advanced social media and Influencer marketing strategy. You should feel proud of yourself.

Being overwhelmed is actually a good thing in this instance. I think of it like a copy machine. Imagine you take 100 sheets of paper and you stack them all into the front of the copy machine. It's going to take a little time but eventually that copy machine is going to finish copying every sheet of paper you fed it. Your subconscious brain is the same. You just fed it a lot of sheets of paper and it's going to work on all of it for you in the background, without you consciously having to do anything. It's strategizing your positioning in the marketplace, it's planning what your best Credibility Content will look like, what you'll share in your Connection Content, and all the different ways you'll be able to monetize with the Chat Engine. All this is happening even if you feel a little bit overwhelmed right now. Pretty sweet, huh?

After you've given all this information a day to sink in, I challenge you to go back to each chapter and flip through. See how much you remember. I bet you'll surprise yourself. And if there's anything you don't remember, that's OK. This is your book. You can go back and re-read any section you want whenever you want.

What should you work on first? Here's what I recommend:

1. Commit to dominating social media. We don't want to aim to compete, we want to aim to dominate. We do this by following Wooden's Rule.

2. Create your AAA and Proof List, and start to share that content using the Credibility Twister.

3. Figure out your Culture and Confessions list, and apply them to your Connection Content using the Connection Twister.

4. Start building out your Chat Engines, one at a time.

This book is a blueprint. Don't read it once and go on with business as usual. I suggest you keep it nearby, and refer to it often. As you start to implement and get feedback, come back to the book and refer to the sections that you feel will help you the most. Immerse yourself in the knowledge. Social media's not going anywhere. It's important you get very comfortable applying these methods. *Keep going!*

WHERE SHOULD WE GO FROM HERE?

I get asked, "Jason, how can I get your help or work with you more closely?" Here are two ways for us to try something together:

1. Recently I set myself a mission to create 100 millionaire students in the next 3 years. To do this, I started mentoring entrepreneurs (including "newbies") every single week on a live training call. Since starting this program, we've helped create 10 new millionaires already (which means I only have 90 more to go!). The cost of the weekly, live mentorship is only $10 a month. If you'd like to get personally mentored by me and maybe even be my next millionaire student, go to JCapitalTraining.com to join me today.

2. If you are an Influencer with more than 100K followers, or you manage the account for an Influencer with more than 100K followers *and* the audience is engaged, I believe you're sitting on a goldmine. I'm really looking to put my Chat Engines to the test and see what we can

do applying them to your business for you. If we partner on this like I have with a few others already, we will do everything, you won't have to lift a finger. My goal is to create a few more great case studies. If you're interested, email me at **Jason@HighStatus.com** with the word "Chat" in the subject line and I'll send you the details.

And that will be the cherry on this sundae.

As you implement what you've learned here, don't worry about any judgement you may or may not get from others.

In the wise words of Emerson, "To be great is to be misunderstood".

I look forward to dominating social media and being "misunderstood" with you :-)

Thank you so much for your time and your energy.

It means the world to me.

Jason Capital